LUCIEN'S STORY

ALEKSANDRA KROH *Translated by Austryn Wainhouse*

T M P

The Marlboro Press/Northwestern
Evanston, Illinois

LUCIEN'S STORY

The Marlboro Press/Northwestern
Northwestern University Press
Evanston, Illinois 60208-4210

Originally published in French under the title *Les Guerres
sont loin*. Copyright © 1993 by Liana Levi et
Éditions du Scribe. English translation copyright ©
1996 by Austryn Wainhouse. Published 1996 by
The Marlboro Press/Northwestern.

Printed in the United States of America

ISBN 0-8101-6020-X   (CLOTH)
ISBN 0-8101-6021-8   (PAPER)

Library of Congress Cataloging-in-Publication Data

Kroh, Aleksandra.
        [Guerres sont loin. English]
        Lucien's story / Aleksandra Kroh ; translated by
Austryn Wainhouse.
                p. cm.
        ISBN 0-8101-6020-X. — ISBN 0-8101-6021-8 (pbk.)
        1. Duckstein, Lucien. 2. Jews—France—
Biography. 3. Holocaust, Jewish (1939–1945)—
France—Biography. 4. France—Ethnic relations. I.
Duckstein, Lucien. II. Title.
DS135.F9D83 1996
940.53'18'092—dc20
[B]   96-22214
                                                CIP

The paper used in this publication meets the
minimum requirements of the American National
Standard for Information Sciences —Permanence
of Paper for Printed Library Materials,
ANSI Z39.48-1984.

Contents

THE BEGINNING

I am eleven years old. Tonight, on this twenty-fifth of November, 1943, I am with my mother in our apartment in Paris, on the rue Francis-le-Pressensé, in the 14th arrondissement, and night is falling. Soon it will be time to go to bed. My father is not with us. Years ago he went off to war with the glorious French Army. They dug trenches near the Maginot Line, they lay in them until the month of May in 1940, and when they heard a shot fired, a single shot, they picked up and marched off. They marched for three days and three nights. The fourth morning they halted because they were already encircled by the Germans.

Since then my father has been a prisoner of war. We write to him each month, and each month we receive word from him. Our letters are censored; all we can say to him is that we are all right, that we love him, that we are hoping to see him again soon. His letters say the same thing to us: that he is all right and hopes to see us again soon. From one letter to another the only thing that changes is the date, which is the only thing that matters: on that date he is alive, we are alive. It is better than nothing.

His way of waging this war is a disappointment to me. I would have preferred him to have halted the Germans, to have prevented them from occupying France. I won't find this out until a lot later, but I'll say it right now: my father doesn't mind it too much in his prisoner of war camp; he is making out all right. The Germans are taken up with getting themselves killed on the Russian front, and it's the women who are cultivating the fields and keeping the factories going. The women manage as best they can, but the machinery doesn't always respond as it should. That's where my father steps in: he repairs the tractors and the harvesters, repairs the radios, the bicycles, the sewing machines and typewriters; he plugs holes, fixes leaks, and replaces fuses. Along with his skills as a mechanic, he speaks fluent German, like every self-respecting Hungarian, and acts as an interpreter when necessary. He is at last declared a bona fide Aryan and receives a certificate to prove it. In this the Germans demonstrate enormous flexibility, for it is quite a feat to recognize the Aryan status of someone named Duckstein, someone who couldn't look less like an Aryan and who would fail the test they employ at the drop of a hat to see whether you are or aren't a Jew. Judge, thereby, the extent to which my father has shown himself useful.

But on the twenty-fifth of November, 1943, he isn't there, he isn't really a part of this story, and he will not be of any help to me in what is to follow, except in one regard, and it is significant: to him I am indebted for my status as the son of a prisoner of war. For among the privileged, none are more privileged than we, the immediate families of prisoners of war. Within our large Hungarian clan, we are the only ones to enjoy the twofold protection provided first of all by our French citizenship and secondly by the uniform my father has worn. If there is some menace hovering in the air, it applies to the others, not to us.

And so it is about the others that we are worried. There was the arrest, last year, of several of my relatives, among them two girl cousins my age, caught in the Vel' d'Hiv' roundup and taken away, without anyone knowing where or what has become of them. Now it is my Aunt Alice who seems to be in danger: she lives with us, but for some time she has been spending the night with friends on the rue Raymond-Losserand, for there has been talk lately of another roundup. This one, according to the rumors we are hearing, is imminent. They will be collecting foreigners only; they won't bother anyone who is French, and especially not anyone who has a prisoner of war in the family. That's what we hear; therefore, that's what we believe, confident that we ourselves are not being targeted.

My cousin Madeleine's parents have carried prudence to the point of taking refuge in the Unoccupied Zone, in Murat, a little town in the Cantal below Clermont-Ferrand. As if this were not enough, they have become Catholics, go to church every Sunday, and Madeleine has made her first communion. I spent all of last August there during the vacation, the one time since the start of the war that I had been outside of Paris. I didn't have the right to do that, of course, but my mother put me on the train with a letter from my aunt in my pocket: "I hereby certify that Lucien Duckstein is my nephew and that I have invited him to spend the summer vacation with me at my home." The train traveled slowly, there was a thorough inspection when we entered the free zone, and I did not feel very comfortable; but, strange to say, thanks to the letter from my aunt, they didn't bother me. I spent the month of August with my cousin, with the local youngsters. I played with them, did all sorts of silly things; like them I went to church, I learned to recite Catholic prayers, to put tadpoles and frogs in the holy water. And once the summer vacation ended, I returned to Paris to enter the lycée.

The children of prisoners of war are entitled to special treatment: once a month they receive restaurant coupons. Ordinarily I go, by myself or with a schoolmate, to one of the little neighborhood restaurants, where I eat a questionable horsemeat steak and fried potatoes. But one time I had a coupon for the restaurant at the corner of the boulevard Montparnasse and the boulevard Raspail, a good restaurant. I went to it alone. Through the window I watched the number 91 buses, the only line that goes by there: buses with enormous roofs because they are powered by gas generators. I ate a salad of leeks, which I am very fond of, and as the leeks had gone bad, I got terrible indigestion.

In short, 1943 hasn't been a brilliant year, but it isn't worse, and there's no reason why it should be worse, than the one before. No, I am not living in fear, I have yet to become a hunted animal. At this point the fear is only latent; rather, it is constraint I feel. The pressures are added one by one, we barely have time to get used to the latest of them when we come under a new one, and we accustom ourselves to that one, too. You must do this, you mustn't do that. First you have to report the possession of any radio you own. Next we find out that Jews do not have the right to have a radio, and, Jewish or not Jewish, nobody has the right to listen to broadcasts from London. We hold on to our radio even so, and we listen to London, with the volume turned down to a whisper, with water running from a tap, knowing that we risk being turned in. So it is that we hear about the landing in North Africa and about Stalingrad.

One day we are apprised that sewing machines have to be handed in; but how are we to do that? My mother is a milliner; how will she be able to work? Consequently, she keeps her sewing machine, continues to make hats, and in exchange for them obtains all sorts of things. She's good at this, so we have enough to eat.

The curfew is instituted. Jews are not allowed to be in the metro after eight at night. We are also forbidden to leave Paris or the nearer suburbs.

And above all, the yellow star must be worn. Just like my mother, sometimes I wear it and sometimes I don't. I am always apprehensive when out in the street: if I wear my star, I am marked, I am exposed, and if I do not wear it, something may happen to me for that very reason. Therefore, I sometimes wear it hidden underneath my jacket, sometimes I display it openly, sometimes I prefer not to have it on me. My school-teacher, a good guy, tells me not to wear it, saying there's no reason why I should. I don't wear it at school.

My mother takes risks also. To get flour she goes to Corbeil, where the big mills are. We are rationed; everyone is entitled to a certain amount of flour and that's all. I always sense my mother's anxiety before she makes this trip. I absorb her fear even if she tries to hide it. Before going to Corbeil she removes her star. She does not have the right to set foot outside Paris, she does not have the right to buy flour on the black market, she does not have the right to be out after the curfew. For five kilos of flour she defies all those prohibitions and risks her skin. In the event of a raid, she wouldn't stand a chance.

The feeling of oppression is permanent, for you see them everywhere: the German women in gray uniforms, those soldiers and officers belonging to the Wehrmacht, or worse still, the SS. But you learn to live in this atmosphere. You become used to it. It ceases to be a surprise that things worsen by the day, that there is this heavy atmosphere, these indiscriminate arrests in the metro, in the streets, everywhere.

At the same time, I am not wanting for attention. I have a loving family, I have uncles and aunts, beginning with Aunt Alice, my favorite. A few weeks ago a great event took place: I was accepted into the beginning year at the Lycée Buffon. Thanks to the competitive examination I took before the vacation (I hadn't put on my star the day of the examination), I was awarded a scholarship, a small scholarship, about a hundred francs a month. I am a good student. I am happy, and I am excited about learning Latin and English. That's it, my daily round: go to the lycée every morning, do my homework every evening. The life I am leading seems pretty normal to me; at any rate, it's the only one I know.

I have some white mice. I keep them in a cage. A bunch of little mice have just been born and there's a great to-do in the mouse family. I feed them, I clean the cage, I could spend the whole night just watching the tiny baby mice.

Had we a crystal ball to see into the future, we would leave this apartment before night comes, we would follow in my Aunt Alice's footsteps, we would spend the night of November 25 with her, at the home of friends. We would leave right away. But since the crystal ball is not there, we spend a very quiet evening, an evening like so many others. My mother does perhaps fret about Alice, but, worrywart that she is, my mother frets about everybody and everything under the sun, always predicting the worst, and I have long since ceased to pay any attention to her forebodings. Radio London speaks of very faraway battles. It is hard to understand what is going on, but it is clear that something is, that something is afoot. My mother is straightening, tidying, she is busy. I bid my mice a very good night and I go to bed rather early, as is right and proper, because tomorrow morning I must go to the lycée; I know that if I am called on I'll do well.

In the middle of the night I am awakened by a racket. There's a banging on the door, someone telling us to open up. My mother does not move, we hold our breath—for if we keep still, won't they go away? But the concierge knows perfectly well that we are there, he says so: "Madame Duckstein," he says, "open the door right away, no foolishness, open up or the door will be broken down." And what with all that shouting and the pounding, my mother unlocks the door. She opens it, and the effect upon us is almost one of relief, for one more second of having to live with that menace on the other side of the door would not have been endurable.

There are two of them, the concierge and a French cop. "Gather a few of your things," the cop says to my mother. "You have fifteen minutes to get yourself ready, then you're coming with me. But you don't have anything to worry about, it's not going to take long."

Fifteen minutes, that's not much. My mother's movements become more deliberate, more efficient as she dresses and gets together the few odds and ends she will take with her. She is strangely calm; she has a firm hold upon that "it's not going to take long." With a fixed expression on her face, she avoids looking at me. She moves quickly, compliantly, so as not to irritate the cop, who is growing impatient. Then they all disappear, and I remain there alone.

It is the middle of the night, but no one in the building is asleep. They awakened everybody with their ruckus. Once they are gone, doors open, neighbors appear on the landings, exchange glances. The neighbor from upstairs comes down. "Lucien," he asks me, "you need anything? Anything I can do?"

"Yes," I tell him, "take my mice. Please take good care of my mice."

"Why sure," he says, "I'll do that."

He stands there looking at me for a moment, hesitates a little, then takes the mice and goes away. I, for my part, go back to bed. If he came down to console me, then he came down for nothing. I don't need consoling. If he is really trying to be of help to me, then it's also for nothing— to help me is something he cannot do, he isn't strong enough. My destiny and his are different destinies, our histories do not blend.

I am only eleven years old, but I am already habituated to petty meannesses, to prohibitions, to constraints, and to risks you take because not taking them could be even riskier. I have already known humiliation. On that fare you grow up fast.

All alone in this apartment, I am bewildered by what is befalling me. My mind is empty. I do not know how I ought to react to what is happening, how afraid I should be, so out of the ordinary the whole business is. And I have no idea what the next chapter will be, I do not know what to expect.

Should I do something? Not do anything? Is there anything to be done? It does not enter my head to put on my clothes, to go up to the neighbors on the floor above and ask them to let me sleep there tonight. Still less does it occur to me to run away, to run off into the darkness outside, into the rain, to seek refuge with my Aunt Alice. No, I do not even look for a way out of the situation. For I already know, I take it for granted, that they are picking up adults only, and consequently I have no cause for panic. I wait for morning to come, I wait for it to be time to go to school. I shall attend class in the usual way, and only afterward shall I go and join Aunt Alice. And then, who knows, perhaps my mother will be back that same evening. Or else her absence will last two or three days, surely not more than that.

I am anxious all the same. I am unable to fall asleep. Huddled under my blankets, having my eyes open is no better than having them shut. It is possible, after all, that they will come back to get me, anything is possible. In that case, they will detain us for several days, but sooner or later they will release us, for my father is a prisoner of war. Even if we have been turned in, we haven't done anything wrong, they'll release us. Anyhow, they themselves said it didn't amount to anything, it was just a verification of identity.

I shall one day be a grown man and free of anxieties, I shall be protected by the law, I shall have nothing to fear, from anyone. The world about me shall be benevolent, I shall rove it from one end to the other, I shall cross borders without even noticing it. I shall change hemispheres, climates, and seasons without any particular emotion. I shall dare to take all sorts of gambles, embark upon all sorts of adventures. I shall be looked up to, waited upon, greeted with kindness. I shall have a fine place in a brightly shining sun. I shall have children, two boys and a girl, who will grow up and become adults without knowing anything—without having the faintest idea—of what I am going through at this moment. They will live in a sunny, luminous land. Their sky will always be blue. Rain for them will be a rare and pleasant distraction. Their animals will be free to run about, their plants will be great powerful cactuses with arms flung toward heaven. Their bodies will be enveloped in warmth. Their house will be spacious. They will enjoy every right and will have no cause to envy anyone. They will suffer from no injustice, they will undergo neither privations nor dangers. Their horizon will be infinite; their view will extend to distant mountains.

I shall discover then, and for me this discovery shall be like a slap in the face, that they know the taste of my ancient fear, that within them there lives the eleven-year-old child who dares not stir in his bed, that they feel themselves neither protected nor supported, and that, no more than I do on the night of the twenty-fifth to twenty-sixth of November, 1943, they do not know what to do about the plight they are in. For without ever having spoken to them about it, I have transmitted to them the confusion and weakness that grip me today. That this something I have wanted to keep to myself, like a mask of infamy, will make of me a father unlike other fathers, different from the one they would have wished to have. And inasmuch as they will not know what it is, they will not be able either to combat it or to accept it. They will only undergo it.

The silence in this apartment has become truly dreadful. But when you come down to it, I am already beginning to say to myself that the silence is just one thing more—and that's enough for it to become a new dispensation, a new norm. Little by little I settle down within it, and I get myself ready for, I await whatever is to follow. Just a little longer and I shall learn how to live with it, to sleep with it. I do not, however, have time to fall asleep, for they return very soon.

"You're to come with your mother, that's how it's going to be, so you too, get some of your stuff together," they say.

I shall find out several days later that for every adult Jew he brings in the inspector receives one hundred francs and fifty francs for every Jewish child. The anger that fills me upon learning that my price is fifty francs will be my first great anger, and the hatred my first great hatred.

He hardly so much as looks at me during the fifteen minutes he allows me to collect my things, and I don't look at him much either; nor do I look at the concierge whom I have known for years and years, to whom I have said hello every morning, who has always replied "Hello, Lucien." But what I learn about that pair will never be forgotten. What I read upon their faces will pursue me for the rest of my life. Looking at some particular person, a thought will cross my mind: you over there, you'd collaborate the first chance you got. There will be no knowing whether I'm right or wrong; but in France and in the United States and in Germany, while dining at the home of friends, during gatherings of all sorts, sometimes very official ones, on vacations, in airplanes and on trains, the idea will come to me: you have a collaborator's mentality, you have the baseness, you have the qualities of a collaborator, you have the look of a collaborator. I'll clink glasses with those people, I'll laugh at their jokes, I'll shake their hand if they extend it to me, all the while thinking: you would write anonymous letters, you would sell your neighbor for fifty francs. You would send me to my death for fifty francs, and even for a lot less, and you'd do it without giving a shit.

The neighborhood police station is a stone's throw from our building.

There I find my mother and many others besides, all only half-awake, all with fear in their weary eyes. We wait, uncertain what we are waiting for. What does that actually mean, a roundup? People get arrested, and after that certain among them are taken somewhere—but where? Off to a labor camp, probably in Germany, to do forced labor—while others, we perhaps, are released.

We ask a policeman what is going to happen to us. "I don't know," he says. "There'll be a bus coming to get you." Around dawn he hands out hot chocolate to the kids, coffee to the grown-ups.

Climbing aboard the bus, I still do not know what is happening to me. I continue to think that real misfortune only happens to others, not to me. The bus makes the rounds of the police stations. Our apartment remains silent and empty; our building wakes up, trying to efface the nighttime commotion from its memory; my schoolmates head off to the Lycée Buffon; people are walking in the streets, but we are no longer part of the crowd. The bus concludes its tour, drives out of Paris without leaving any traces behind, and proceeds toward—we eventually find out—Drancy. We disappear as if we had never existed. We already know that this is something other than a simple verification of identity.

And so, after the next bend in the road, it shall be Drancy. But of what Drancy will be like, and of what we are going to discover around the ensuing bends, we have not the faintest idea.

WAITING

It is a former military barracks, an immense rectangular building full of stairwells, with a big courtyard in the center. We are about a hundred persons, women and children, in a dormitory on the third floor. The dormitory is heated; we are cold only in the latrines, which are located outside, at the other end of the camp, barracks latrines from the beginning of the century, planks with holes.

Around the barracks is some vacant land and, farther off, the towers, the barbed-wire fences, the armed guards. Behind you see blocks of low-income housing and a little road upon which every now and then you see people walking. How lucky they are to be free to come and go, we say to ourselves.

We are lodged at the entrance to the camp, opposite the main gate. Not far from us live those who are one-eighth or one-quarter Jewish. We even have a song:

> *How many Jewish, half-Jewish, quarter-Jewish*
> *Jewish Jewish grandmothers have you got*
> *Who wouldn't eat fried bacon, wouldn't eat fried bacon?*
> *How many Jewish, half-Jewish, quarter-Jewish*
> *Jewish Jewish grandfathers have you got*
> *Who weren't circumcised, who weren't circumcised?*

The Drancy camp is merely for people in transit. Nothing special happens at Drancy. There is not enough to eat, there are lice, cockroaches, above all there is diarrhea, from time to time somebody dies, but not in our building and in any case it's pretty rare. Otherwise, nothing important, over a period of six months. As is her wont, my mother anticipates the worst. She does, of course, look after me as best she can; she watches over me, protects me. She tells me ten times a day there is nothing for me to be worried about, meanwhile heaving sighs and asking her God what has befallen us and what else there is in store for us. For my own part, all I do is wait. I truly do not feel at all anxious.

Newcomers arrive in the big room we occupy, nothing but wives and children of prisoners of war; instead of a hundred we are now one hundred and fifty, then two hundred, and soon still more. It is becoming difficult.

Drancy is only somewhere on the way to somewhere else. Drancy is a purgatory. In Paris we were free to move about, free for a time, for deep down we knew that something else was in the offing. The atmosphere in Paris was good preparation for Drancy. We have already become accustomed to thinking that things are not going to improve, that, to the contrary, the future can only be worse. To us it seems normal to be heading downhill, ever farther down; and whatever happens comes to us as no surprise.

We have only just left normal life; we are still in greater Paris, after all. Newcomers arrive bringing fresh news. The best informed are those who had been working at Lévitan's, a Jewish-owned furniture store: those who had been clearing out the apartments of arrested Jews, sorting the paintings, the objets d'art, the furnishings, packing them up and shipping them off to Germany.

We tell ourselves that that's all it comes down to, to laying hands on the Jews' property, to stripping us clean, perhaps to sending us off to do compulsory labor. We aren't expecting anything worse than that. After all, my father has been a prisoner of war for three years. We send packages to him, he writes to us, we know that he's more or less all right. To us, our situation does not appear particularly tragic or dangerous. We, families of prisoners of war, preserve the crazy hope of soon being set free. Most of us are modest people, and even if we are attached to the things we own, it wouldn't be all that awful to lose everything. We are absolutely incapable of imagining that they also want to take away our life, and our dignity.

We try to grasp what is happening. A bus we refer to as "Paris-Soir" arrives almost every day. It drives in the main entrance, filled with people who have just been arrested, who were out after the curfew or did not have their papers, who were somewhere they shouldn't have been, who weren't wearing the star, who were picked up because of their looks, who were transporting a kilo of butter, or who were unlucky. They tell us what they heard on a Radio London broadcast the other day, they pass on the latest rumors, they report what is going on in Paris and elsewhere. The picture that emerges from this is perhaps not very clear or entirely coherent, but the imagination has been provided something upon which to feed. One has been given grounds for rejoicing if one is an optimist and for tearing one's hair if one is not.

We also see people leave. We try not to do too much wondering about where they are going. Nevertheless, if someone comes out with the question, someone else rejoins: "To the devil." Or, more exactly, to *Pitchipoï*, which is something like that in Yiddish. All we really know is that they go to Pithiviers first and then eastward in sealed freight cars, for there are people who have seen them, who were able to read the destinations inscribed on those freight cars, and who know that those trains sometimes go to Germany, sometimes to Poland, bound for unfamiliar places, localities no one has ever heard of. Probably, we tell ourselves, this has to do with compulsory labor, perhaps particularly hard labor; but we do not suspect anything worse.

We observe that those they put in the building adjoining the main entrance are taken away the following morning in dozens of buses. We observe that men are always very quick to leave. We see convoys depart every Saturday. We see buses come in to collect people and then come back empty to get others. Over the course of six months we see a convoy set out once or twice each week.

From time to time, but very rarely, someone is released. That means that he has managed to prove that he has under 25 percent Jewish blood in his veins, that he is less than a quarter Jew.

Relationships are vertical, between the mothers and the children. Although there are quite a few youngsters my age, there is no question of making friends, no question of building a world of personal attachments. For here in Drancy what is beginning to come to the fore is not always the good side of human nature, and it is not always pretty to behold. Certainly it is better not to be alone, better to have someone to talk to, to play with, but friendship does not interest me, I am not looking for any. What is in my best interest is self-centeredness, to attend first of all to my own affairs. That indeed is the first thing I learn in Drancy.

The first thing, but not the only thing. We live on top of each other, women and children crammed together. Most of the women have been living without a man, have been deprived of a man, for two or three years. That is what they talk about now, about their desires and their projects. They go farther and farther in their anecdotes, the details they give are more and more intimate. Their stories are true or sheer fantasy, it's the same thing, for what they say is said in a very direct manner, in language that could not be more explicit, and their jokes are truly crude—the more so because the women here are of all sorts. The most entertaining is Fernande, formerly a hawker of fruits and vegetables on the rue Saint-Denis, doubtless somewhat of a prostitute as well. It's an excellent education for an eleven-year-old boy. It's highly interesting and pretty shocking at the same time. In words and in gestures, all modesty shortly goes by the board. The women discuss their sexual organs as if they were talking about the tips of their noses. They reach into their underwear, they adjust, they remove, they wash their sanitary napkins in broad daylight, indifferent to the presence of the children. You soon no longer even notice it.

In Drancy I learn, too, how important it is to remain upright, to use one's head, to find things to do. I see people refuse to sink into passivity and who, insofar as is possible, try to keep active. They organize evening get-togethers, performances, variety shows that take place in the big room on the second floor, which seems to have once been a school classroom. Among us there is a singer, there is a mime. The indefatigable Fernande sings in her raucous and vulgar voice, all the while prancing about, lifting her skirt. Then, disguised as a man, she dances with another woman, who acts the whore; the love scene they put on is a perfect riot. Seen with the eyes of a young boy, it is very diverting indeed.

Yes, at Drancy we are still altogether human. We continue to try to hold on to certain things, to keep our heads up. There are people who continue to think that it is natural to give children an education. A rabbi has been teaching us to sing in Hebrew, but he leaves very soon. I start learning Yiddish, because Yiddish is what the women speak with one another. There are many, above all those from Central Europe, whose French is not very good. From time to time someone comes forth with a piece of good advice, explains how to behave when you are hungry or have stomach pains. Someone taught me one day that when you have diarrhea, stay on the pot until you urinate for the second time; after that you can get up. It's something very useful to know.

And especially, and above all, there's Loève.

His wife is Catholic, so is he, but he has Jewish forebears and someone reported him; nevertheless, he hopes to be able to get out, for he is a little less than a quarter Jewish. In the meantime—I know not where or how— he has got hold of a blackboard and some chalk, and every morning, from ten until noon, he teaches us algebra. A dozen of us make up his class.

From ten o'clock until twelve I forget about everything else.

Loève is an absolutely remarkable teacher. I have no way of knowing it, but he is a great French mathematician, a familiar name to all those interested in probability. That he is teaching algebra to eleven-year-old kids is something incredible, something unheard of, and for us it is an enormous stroke of luck and a great honor.

The memory of those lessons will remain with me forever. He explains algebra to us as if he were performing magic. He believes in algebra, and, with him, immediately, we too become believers in it. Before my eyes algebra becomes transparent as crystal. Train A sets out to meet train B coming toward it; reservoirs fill with clear water. He offers us a problem to solve as if it were a gift, and we appreciate its value. All my life I shall take refuge in algebra as an antidote to bleak thoughts, I shall calm myself by summoning to mind a problem to solve; all my life mathematics will have for me the power to dispel anxiety and sorrow. Mathematics will occupy an important place in my life. It is here, in Drancy, that I learn to love mathematics, thanks to Professor Loève.

That goes on for about three months, at the end of which they let him go. Good for him. One day he moves out of the quarter-part-Jew neighborhood, to our great joy, although it is hard on us to lose him. He is set free along with the others who have been able to prove that they aren't all that Jewish.

Until the end of the war he will keep pretty much out of sight, for with that just under a quarter part of Jewish blood of his, he won't be entirely safe. Afterward he will emigrate to the United States. He will enter Berkeley by the front door. He will only have say "My name is Loève" for them to reply, "Fine, your professor's chair is waiting for you." He will publish books, one of which, *Probability Theory,* will become a classic, a landmark. The book will be written in English, of course, but the dedication will be in French: "To the children of the camp at Drancy."

Learning of that I shall feel very proud, proud to think that he had not forgotten us. "Perhaps," I shall say to myself, "perhaps we brought him something in return." The thought itself will give me enormous pleasure, for both as a man and as a mathematician I shall have been influenced more by Loève than by any other of my many teachers. He shall have marked me for life. I shall always remember certain phrases, certain formulations of his; I could quote them word for word. Without Loève, I would perhaps have chosen an altogether different direction, had an altogether different destiny; for one day, following psychotechnical tests and a handwriting analysis, a psychologist will tell me that I was cut out to be a writer and had no true bent for mathematics. That may be so after all. But to know a teacher like Loève, a scientist like Loève, is to be impregnated for life with the desire to teach and to do research, and I was never to consider doing anything else.

Thirty years later, when I, too, had become a professor of applied mathematics at an American university, I went to visit Loève in Berkeley. I looked him up in the telephone book, I called him, and he remembered me; he told me to come right out. Oh yes, he recognized me, and for my part I found him no less marvelous than the man I had stood in such awe of at Drancy. To meet again was something of an experience for both of us.

He was to be very happy in Berkeley. There he found an incomparable intellectual ambience, for Berkeley is a paradise for those of us who do science. He was highly prized there, very well remunerated, his teaching obligations were few, he was at liberty to do whatever he pleased. In Berkeley's great libraries he found all the world's books; he had as many research assistants and as many students as he wanted, not just the average sort, but outstanding students, for Berkeley attracted the best there were. His students would gaze at him in wonder and would drink up his words, just as we were doing now. He would stroll in the sunshine on Berkeley's flower-filled campus, among the sequoias, the eucalyptus, the magnolias. And he would die in the 1980s, much regretted.

Yes, at Drancy we are yet very human. Drancy will not have broken us. The mindless will have remained mindless, the downcast will have remained downcast, the noble will have remained noble. The story of Drancy is not as extraordinary as all that.

In any case, the time came to leave.

If they held us in Drancy for as long as they did, it is because we were the families of prisoners of war. That is why we were placed so far from the main gate. But one day—the third of May, 1944—our turn came.

Our convoy was made up of three hundred persons: two hundred fifty women and children who had been sent to Drancy between the end of 1942 and the eve of our departure, and the fifty women without children who had worked at the Lévitan warehouse and who had only just arrived. The fifty women had been living in Paris, assigned to residence in a kind of ghetto, taken to and from work under escort. They were as good as prisoners but a little better treated, better fed than we had been in Drancy. And they were in far better physical shape.

In the earliest hours of the morning, buses transport us to the Gare de l'Est. It is very cold in Paris that day. Frozen, clutching our bundles, we stand for a long time in front of the station. We wait, we wait, and I can see the boulevard de Strasbourg, wrapped in morning mist, extending all the way to Châtelet. It's not especially cheerful, there's little traffic, the few pedestrians are all in a hurry. I gaze at the boulevard de Strasbourg, and I wonder when I'll see it again, when I'll be able to run along its sidewalks, to go toward the Seine, to look at it, to go still farther. I wonder when I'll be free again, like others. Owing to all I heard said and not said in Drancy, I think that we are going to be sent to a camp, probably in Germany. I think this without thinking about it very much; I am weary and I am cold.

They put us in third-class carriages. This may not be a bad sign; we know that the others left in sealed freight cars, whereas we are seated in normal compartments, even if there are twelve of us in each of them and not eight.

We do not know where we are being taken. There is nothing marked on the outside of our carriage, nothing at all. It is an ordinary carriage hitched to an ordinary train.

Late in the afternoon the train gets under way and heads due east.

BERGEN-BELSEN

We travel for all of a day, for all of a night. Our carriage is maneuvered from time to time; it is disconnected from one train in order to be hooked onto another, something that we note but refrain from commenting upon. Coming to Düsseldorf we witness a frightful air raid. We stop and are taken down to a cellar underneath the station, and there, in the shelter, waiting for the attack to end, this bombing gladdens us. We rejoice to see the fear, the helpless terror written upon those German faces. These bombs are not of great concern to us: we know that they are not intended for us, that it's not us they are seeking to destroy.

We could even take advantage of this panic and confusion in order to escape; but after that what would we do, in this Germany in the year 1944, where would we go with our appearance of deportees? And so we obediently climb aboard the train again, we resume our journey toward the unknown. Between Hanover and Hamburg, at a place called Celle, we get off, and after two or three kilometers on foot we reach Bergen-Belsen.

As the name *Bergen-Belsen* is uttered, I see a veritable mask of horror settle upon the faces of the women. I do not know how or from whom, but they must have heard about this camp. What mood does it produce in me to behold that expression on their faces? It makes little difference; from now on moods are things I no longer have. I already know, or intuit, that unduly strong emotions can be fatal. As if it were something I had been taught in school, I know that here there is no room for moods.

Dictionaries do not contain words enough to talk about Bergen-Belsen. Here, to say *hunger* or *fear* is to burden those words with an intensity for which they were not conceived, to give them a dimension they are unable to assume; it is to be unable to use them ever again outside of Bergen-Belsen. It is never to be able to say *I'm hungry* when lunch is late being put on the table, when one arrives in the evening in a small country town where one doesn't know a soul and all the restaurants have closed. If I utter the word *fear* in Bergen-Belsen, I shall never be able to employ it to describe what one feels on the eve of taking an important exam, or while driving at night in dense fog with headlights that are not working well. However, I shall have need of these words and of so many others, for I shall survive, I shall survive what is going to follow, and I cannot, after all, without seeming pedantic or pretentious, explain each time that, properly speaking, all I am referring to is a faint hollowness in the stomach or a sort of vague disquiet.

The smarter thing, no doubt, would be to let words retain their former meaning, the meaning they are invested with for ordinary use in a normal world, and to invent a new vocabulary all my own for Bergen-Belsen, with words never seen hitherto, unpronounceable and dreadful, such as, let's say, *schwryhrkrtz* or *uuuuup* or whatever, moan-words, scream-words. But I didn't think of that in time, I have had other things on my mind; and so the words that I know will first be too weak for Bergen-Belsen and after that too strong for any other reality. Either way, I shall communicate my feelings poorly, and I won't do much to remedy it.

We are walking across a wooded plain. We are walking through a splendid, majestic forest of firs, dark, almost black. As we near the camp, we encounter a sickening odor, an odor of scorched pig. We are still very naive, for, of course, the stench has nothing to do with pigs. Human corpses are being burned.

Here again is the concentration camp world, with its watchtowers and its barbed-wire fences. Upon our arrival, we all have our heads shaved, women and children, to protect us against lice, we are told. Our hair is carefully collected, probably for the manufacture of mattresses. The women wear turbans, seeking to protect their bare skulls and to hide their ugliness.

At Drancy we had succeeded in keeping a few precious items—jewels, watches, brooches, souvenirs; for some we had found hiding places. At Bergen-Belsen that is over with. Everybody removes his clothes and we hand over everything, everything, including the three or four coins still left in our pockets. And we obtain receipts: this one for three francs and seventy centimes, that one for a wedding ring. Detailed description, date, rubber stamp, signature. Since then, whatever its prowess, bureaucracy no longer has the capacity to astonish me.

All of us, women and children, are put in a hut. It is infinitely less comfortable than our Drancy dormitory, yet it compares very favorably with what we will come to know later on. Our beds are stacked in tiers: there are two tiers at the outset, which will shortly give way to three, and toward the end to four. There are not enough beds to go around, and I sleep with my mother.

The women are put to work at once. My mother sorts the clothing and footwear presumably coming here from other camps. She is taken aback and horrified to see so much of it. She cuts off the least worn parts of the clothes and recuperates bits and pieces of leather, particularly the soles of old shoes. Other women deal with jewelry and gold teeth, thousands of jewels and teeth pass through their hands. After a time my mother opens silkworm cocoons, unwinds the silk, puts it in a sack. The skin on her hands is cut by the knife, by the silk thread.

The women go off to work every morning. While waiting for their mothers to return the children wander about aimlessly, pick up pebbles, wait for the roll call to be taken. Every day we must remain standing while they count us. We report the number of sick; we say there are eleven of them, but sometimes that is not the correct figure, there are fewer than that, or more, someone has changed his mind at the last moment, has come out for the roll call instead of staying in the hut, or vice versa. They, too, sometimes make mistakes in their counts. Then everything has to be done all over again; it is endless. It's a relief to wind up with the exact number, to reach the end of the roll call.

We have real hunger now, not like the hunger we had during the period at Drancy. For the whole day we have a little chunk of bread and a serving of soup, this being water with a few bits of rutabaga in it. Rutabaga is a delicacy, a treat in Bergen-Belsen. I eat rutabaga soup for eleven and a half months.

They say we are getting a bare six hundred calories a day, while normally it requires a minimum of two thousand to keep alive. My mother scrabbles as best she can. She literally takes the bread from her own mouth in order to give it to me. Sometimes she returns from work with a little piece of rutabaga or a bit of a potato for me. If she chances upon a cigarette butt, she exchanges it for a piece of bread. For there are some who prefer a butt to a piece of bread, and among them certain ones will survive on this regimen.

There are two whores in our hut. One of them is even several cuts above a whore. She formerly directed a brothel in Paris on the rue Blondel, and she was arrested after her pimp turned her in for having hidden a Jew or someone in the Resistance. Both women sleep with the Germans. Not only do they eat fairly well themselves, they even contrive to bring back food for the children, or else return with cigarettes that can be traded for food. In general everyone is grateful to them, but there are women here and there who insult them. Berthe, who will later become our friend, treats them with respect. "You are really very nice," the brothel-keeper said to Berthe one day. "When the war's over, send your husband round, I'll give him the prettiest girl in the house." Berthe said thank you.

Being hungry: It's waiting for the food, waiting for it all the time, never ceasing to wait for it. When the food arrives, it's managing to get the serving at the bottom of the pot, down there where there may be a few extra pieces of rutabaga. Managing, that means being the victor in the fight, because everybody wants to get the bottom of the pot, that means outsmarting the others. It's cutting off a little piece of bread from one's little piece of bread in order to stash it away, in order to hide it under the tick. Being hungry: It's to be filled with hatred, with pain, with an indescribable despair when this little cache is stolen, which happens to me the way it happens to everybody else. And like everybody else, I become very skillful at hiding my bread. Being hungry: It's taking your tin plate and going to sit down on your bed with your back turned to the others, sometimes even getting under the covers so that those who have already finished can't see that you are still eating, and so as not to see others eating when you yourself have nothing left to eat.

On certain days there is no soup at all, no bread, there is nothing; they have probably forgotten us, or else it's something they do for the fun of it. At such times, the little piece of bread you are keeping in reserve is of a value beyond all imagining.

Hunger is an obsession. Ten, twenty, forty years afterward I shall not be able to bear feeling hungry; even mild hunger will throw me into a panic, will make me completely lose my head, will make me aggressive and irritable. I shall not wait for the meal, I shall have to eat something right away—an apple, a sandwich, a piece of chocolate, anything. I shall not be able to put up with the feeling of hunger.

We promise ourselves that, once out of here, we shall eat mountains of rutabagas. We dream of thick rutabaga soups, of tremendous rutabaga dishes prepared in a thousand different ways, seasoned with a rich beet sauce, with first-class margarine. We become crazy from talking about rutabaga, talking about it endlessly.

About potatoes we dare not even dream.

THE WINTER

The winter of 1944–45 is terribly cold. The temperature descends to fifteen below zero, twenty below, and we are ill-clad and ill-fed. Because of diarrhea, there are those who have spent the night in the latrines. Some die there. In the morning they are found frozen, crumpled; commandos pick them up and haul them away in carts.

We have changed huts several times, and each time there are fewer of us to make the move. We are no longer three hundred but between two hundred and two hundred fifty. Our present hut is about twenty-five meters long by ten meters wide. It is unheated. To have water we melt snow. You can barely make your way between our beds, which are now stacked four high. The best places are the uppermost ones, for two reasons: first, it's warmer up there, and second, you have only your own lice, while if you are on the bottom tier you end up with those that fall from the beds above you. You have to wait in order to obtain a spot on the fourth tier. You rise as those at the top die one by one.

We put up curtains against the cold.

With all the lice, the fleas, and the roaches, there is typhus, naturally. Very soon after our arrival, a German doctor took all the children and gave them a big injection in the chest. It hurt a great deal. Subsequently certain kids developed typhus, but they might have caught it anyhow.

The man has gone on with his injections. We try to hide from him: sometimes we succeed, sometimes we don't. Altogether I've had three or four injections. It's not clear to me whether he is experimenting on us or whether it's really to prevent typhus.

Generally when one gets typhus there's nothing to be done; recoveries are rare. The sick are put in the infirmary, where they die very quickly. One day I, too, have a fever, though not a big fever; I do not know whether it is typhus or something else; I am put in the infirmary among the men. It is warm there. However, I am unable to sleep, for all night long there are people dying, and some of them make such a business of it that I regret not being in our hut, even if it is so awfully cold. One evening a very religious Dutchman begins to die and starts praying. He prays all night, and at dawn he is still there doing his praying and his yelling. I am in a bed just above him, and my one wish is that he die as quickly as possible, that he pass on into his better world and that I finally be allowed to go to sleep. Were I a believer, I, too, would probably begin to pray, to pray that he die at once. But I am not a believer. Not anymore.

In this camp there are some very devout Jews who pray all day long, which does not prevent some among them from contracting typhus and disappearing in short order. Some will survive and will thank God for having saved them. And I see with my own eyes that religion has no importance, that the only things that count are the desire to survive and perhaps luck. Among the people I see survive there are some who pray and others who curse God. I tell myself that God has nothing to do with what goes on in Bergen-Belsen. I tell myself that he does not exist. And if he exists, if he allows what is being done to us at Bergen-Belsen, then I don't want to have anything to do with him, I don't want to hear any mention of his name. Never, during the whole of my life, shall I give two hoots about religion. I shall not even be against it; I shall simply not care about it. Nothing said to me on the subject will cause me to change my mind.

Who knows, but for Bergen-Belsen I might have maintained some sort of bond with religion, I would not have rejected it to the point of becoming oblivious to it. I might perhaps have found it moving to watch my mother light candles on Friday evenings. I would have accompanied her to the synagogue now and then. For without being fanatic or even truly strict, my mother respects tradition and will always continue to do so. At Bergen-Belsen she continues to pray, and it is to God she address-es the greater part of her interminable complaints. I cannot say that when I see her praying I shrug my shoulders—for I have no energy to put into shruggings of shoulders—but inwardly that's what it amounts to.

But it will be come a more complex business later on, for I shall live and bring up my children in the United States, where the instructions will be to "give them a religion to believe in." A religion, a faith of whatever sort. It will be all right to be Protestant or Jewish or Catholic; if none of those will suffice, then Mormon, Seventh-Day Adventist, Jehovah's Witness, an adept of whatever you please. But it will not be all right to be nothing at all. "Let them be given a faith." It will be trumpeted every-where, and it will be incumbent upon parents to propose their religion to their offspring, to say to them: "That's my religion. Try believing in it yourself. If you don't want to, well, that'll be your problem, but give it a shot." And the parents will comply with the instructions.

But I, a total agnostic, will have nothing to propose to my kids, noth-ing to give them. I shall be empty-handed. I shall not even be able to give them a hatred of religion, not even that, nothing. That nothing will be too difficult a burden for them to carry. Each in his own way, they will seek out gurus, true believers, spiritual or intellectual guides; they will look for someone who has the answer, who possesses the truth. They will do so because in Bergen-Belsen, at the age of twelve, I decide that God does not exist, and because I shall adhere to that decision all my life. It is a decision I make on my own behalf, for myself alone; I cannot know that I am depriving the children I shall someday have of the freedom to make it for themselves. And were I to know it, that, of course, wouldn't change any-thing at all.

FALLING

As time passes, the women lose everything that make them feminine. They are transformed into bad imitations of women, into caricatures, with their shaved heads, their bellies and breasts that are nothing more than skin. Some become so thin that their vaginas hang outside, their muscles being too weak to hold them in position.

One after the other we lose our reflexes as social beings, and before long we lose our elementary human dignity, with its educated, its civilized aspect. Aggressiveness reigns. The beast takes over. In Bergen-Belsen, the human dimensions waste away.

Everything I was taught in the other life, the one I have left behind me, ceases to have much meaning when one is dying from hunger. *Be nice, be kind, behave properly, make friends, study*—those are words no one employs here. In order not to forget that the rules have changed, it is enough for me to see a huge kapo come running up, a brute with the look of an utter idiot, who wades in, flails about with his club, putting in a greater effort than the Germans ask of him. It's he who supervises the camp; the Germans no longer need bother their heads about it.

I learn to defy prohibitions. I learn not to tell the truth. I learn to hide and not get caught. In Bergen-Belsen, all social rules are at an end. I learn that the one thing that counts is survival, survival and nothing else. Thefts occur every day, and every day there are fights—terrible, violent, bestial. It's the cave man who has wakened in each of us; it's the law of the strongest and of the most cunning that we have to obey. The weak, whether they be weak with themselves or toward others, stand no chance. Weakness of either kind suffices to eliminate you.

I learn to be wary of despondency, of depression, to fight them off with all the strength I have. I see people die when they yield to depression. I can recognize someone who is abandoning hope, and I know that in a few hours he will be done for. I see that if one allows one's will to live to weaken, the end is near. And I say to myself: me, never.

I have got to defend myself, for my mother is a depressive person. I have got to fight against that danger. I have already found out that depression can be contagious. Without my mother, I would be unable to survive, but without me she wouldn't survive either. She would succumb to depression; she would not feel herself obliged to hang on. We support each other mutually.

Later this will be the source of problems for me. I shall be accused of heartlessness, of not understanding. And it is true, I shall not understand, I shall not want to understand. "The mess this house is in depresses me," I shall be told. And I shall reply: "Then tidy it up, what are you waiting for, do something." "But I can't," I shall be told. And I shall not understand what is meant by that.

I shall be told: "I have no wish to live." I shan't understand that either.

It will be explained to me that depression is a sickness like other sicknesses. I shall listen, I shall concede it intellectually, but that's as far as it will go. I shall not understand.

Certain women, my mother among them, never stop complaining, while others who are no less badly off never complain. Lamentations annoy me, that's all.

I learn to be skeptical. I shut myself in. I learn to live from day to day.

Despite everything, we consider ourselves lucky. Bergen-Belsen is a special-treatment labor camp. They have several zones here, one of which is better than ours, the one containing the half-Jews, or something like that. But ours isn't too bad either, the zone for the families of prisoners of war. We are still a privileged group, the French Army continues to protect us a little. We are in a labor camp, and we are expected to work and to die a slow death simply because we do not get enough calories to survive. Anyone who collapses is recycled, but they do not send us alive into the gas chambers. People die from time to time, the bodies are taken to the edge of the camp, then commandos collect them, and that's that. It's extermination through exhaustion; they are not in any hurry to be done with us. With us, the situation is still short of dramatic.

In our zone in addition to ourselves there are some Hungarian Jews, for the Hungarians are allies of the Germans, and above all lots of Dutch people, I don't know why. The Dutch have been dropping all over the place. They die more easily than we do, they have no resistance whatsoever. It's very odd.

We soon find out that we are well above the lowest category, the one that is in the adjoining zone, separated from ours only by a barbed-wire fence. There they put deportees who arrive from Auschwitz and other extermination camps, and the Russian prisoners of war. The latter are treated worse than anyone else.

They do not work, they are not in a state to work; exceptionally they are sent into the forest to look for firewood or to cut down some trees for an extension of the camp. They remain standing all day long in formation, and from time to time one of them falls. If he is able to get up, fine; if not, he is carried off. And then it is another's turn. All day long they wait for them to fall. They collapse without a sound. Then some prisoners who are just as thin as cadavers take hold of them, throw them into a cart, and drag the cart in the direction of the oven. And if one out of every five or six of these prisoners survives, that will be doing very nicely indeed.

One day we observe the arrival of five thousand prisoners, prisoners from all sorts of countries, coming from a variety of concentration camps, all with numbers tattooed on their arms. Despite the rule forbidding it, we try to talk to them through the fence. Some speak Yiddish, others German, French, Polish, Russian, Hungarian too. Those five thousand men are dead in a week. All of them. For the most part they die on their feet, standing at attention. One after the other. The corpses pile up, they are carried away, and at the end of a week there's not one of them left.

You learn to be pretty callous toward the sufferings of others. You have no choice. If you already don't give a great deal of thought to what you yourself are feeling, then as regards others. . . . At any rate, toward the end, we no longer feel anything at all. The question is how to survive, not of knowing what one is feeling. The little energy you have left you do not waste in pity.

We stare at those lined-up Russian prisoners. One keels over, then another. They are picked up. Yet another collapses halfway; he is finished off with a clubbing. They are silent while they are standing, they topple over in silence. At bottom it's a show we're watching, a show all our own. Surely, when every day you see several corpse-filled carts go by, carts drawn by the living dead, you say to yourself—without entirely believing it—that could happen to you, too. But we absolutely cannot feel what those people over there are feeling, nor what we would be feeling if we were safe and sound in some warm place and with our bellies full. Pity is a luxury.

All I know is that I am hungry.

Are they even aware, our Germans, that we are human beings? Doubtless they are not. We are animals. We are numbers. We are two levels below them—there's the category of kapos between them and us.

From time to time an occasional SS will lash some Russian prisoners. It happens also that they pitch into women, but not often; they find the women too disgusting. And so there is no question of their feeling pity or remorse, absolutely not. They are just as unfeeling as we are.

Still, some small amount of solidarity remains, we still retain something human which comes forth from time to time, but reduced to its simplest expression. Mothers protect their children and even the children of others. There are those two prostitutes who bring back food for the kids. There is still a small something, but it is small, very small. And you cannot rely on it, you cannot put your trust in it.

The fifty Lévitan women are an exception to the rule; among them a sense of community continues to exist, they give one another help and support. Forty, maybe forty-two, of them will survive, whereas over half of the others will perish. True, they are fairly vigorous; they had been selected to work at Lévitan's, and after that they were relatively well fed and provided for.

One day I see Berthe having a fight with a woman who does not belong to this group, a woman who is jealous of the solidarity that reigns within it and who takes to calling Berthe names. They begin to fight, and it is no holds barred. While they are certainly not very strong, I am even less so. However, I attempt to separate them, which is a risky thing to do, after all, but which is even more a shocking thing to do, so shocking that they stop and stare at me in surprise. I shall forget this incident; it is Berthe who, forty-nine years later, will relate it to me, and indeed it will come back to me. I shall recall that scene. And I shall consider it altogether to my credit, especially since there is precious little to my credit at Bergen-Belsen, or to the credit of anybody at all.

I see death come amongst us every day, I often look into its eyes, I am able to recognize it from very far off. It does not frighten me; it is nothing at all to me. And thus will it remain. I shall dread having blood samples taken from my veins, I shall dread operations and illnesses. I shall conscientiously do what the doctor prescribes. I shall keep an eye on my cholesterol and sugar levels; I shall not smoke, and I shall be annoyed when others smoke in my presence; I shall pay careful attention to my health. I shall do my best to fend off the old enemy. But it will be on principle and through habit rather than from fear.

I shall always dislike crew cuts, closely cropped hair. I shall go to the barber as infrequently as possible, and I shall always be overtaken by a sort of uneasiness when he bears down on me with his scissors, when I hear that snipping, crackling sound of scissors in contact with my hair. I shall always keep my hair rather on the long side. Fortunately, baldness will never be one of my problems, I shall have an abundant head of hair, I shall never again see the reflection of my unadorned skull. The sight of a bald person will arouse in me a kind of discomfort or a feeling mingling pity and trepidation.

In women I shall like long hair: a halo of curly hair surrounding the face, masses of hair in rich disorder, fine, straight, well-behaved hair shoulder-length and longer. I shall like smooth hair and unruly; I shall adore chignons and ponytails and braids. Among blond, dark, and red hair I shall have no preferences. I shall admire them all simply because they are there, gleaming, stirring with movements of the head, billowing in the wind, being tossed back by a carefree gesture, dancing to the rhythm of footsteps.

When a woman in my entourage cuts her hair, I shall be invaded by an uneasiness, a sorrow from the past. For me it will be as if a part of her person were taken away from her, as if I were in danger of soon having to behold a naked, helpless skull, of having to live once again through the triumph of cruel and pointless ugliness.

NOTHING

We are spending a lot of our time killing lice, fleas, roaches. I learn the way to catch fleas by moistening your fingers. There are crabs, too. Mosquitoes appear the moment winter is over. All those things are flying, crawling, hopping around and upon us, and drinking our blood.

A woman gives birth. She was already pregnant when she was taken to Drancy, and she has her baby in Bergen-Belsen. When it is born, the women say that it makes up for all those that have been dying. The baby lives for three months and that's it.

Fernande is still alive; she is by now greatly diminished, but she is alive and will survive. She is no longer the same Fernande who used to sing songs in Drancy, who would tell her off-color stories, who would perform belly dances for us, and who put her audience in stitches. Here, over the course of all these months, she has not had the energy to attempt a single smile.

One day, on the other side of the fence, we get a glimpse of my mother's Hungarian cousin; after some hide-and-seek with our god-awful kapo, we manage to get close enough to be able to speak to her.

Our sweaters are riddled with holes. We swap them in order not to expose the same parts of ourselves to the cold all the time. It is almost funny.

We do not wash, of course. It stinks in the hut, but the smell doesn't bother us all that much.

We sleep soundly. We are very weak; it's an almost lethargic sleep. Not having eaten anything doesn't keep us from falling asleep, but it is truly disagreeable to wake up with an empty sensation in your stomach and not have anything to put in it.

You don't get accustomed to it. You resign yourself.

I live with whatever comes along, without trying to understand. I am, after all, a child. I do not have many points of reference. I haven't had much experience. In Paris I may have gone as far as the Pont de Sèvres or the Pont de Saint-Cloud once or twice; otherwise I never went outside my little 14th arrondissement. I have made one trip to the Massif Central and that's all. For me the world is what I see around me right now. I have a feeling of injustice rather than anything else, maybe a feeling of anger, when I think there are people who are living normally, who above all are eating normally.

There are all sorts of women among us, some of them cultivated and intelligent women who no doubt have read good books, listened to beautiful music, led intellectually active lives, women who have had a rich past, full of different adventures, who have loved people and known faraway countries. All that has been left behind. For eleven and a half months our imagination has limited itself to food. We think about food and about nothing else. We are vegetating. We pass our time waiting, first of all for our soup, and then for our diarrhea to stop, for the cold weather to end, for things to become still worse, just waiting.

Eleven and a half months: that's a long time. During those eleven and a half months I have waited, I have killed lice, and I have been hungry. Whenever I so much as move my little finger my hunger reawakens. Sometimes they put the boys in with the men, sometimes with the women. Every day it is worse than the day before and better than tomorrow. That's the way the time passes.

There's nothing anywhere, nothing. A complete vacuum, nothingness everywhere. Intellectual, moral nothingness, emptiness in the stomach, total absence of news. No intellectual activity at all. We still receive letters once a month, eleven all told from my father and two from my Aunt Alice. They are happy moments, even if there really isn't anything in those letters. That's all I read in the course of eleven and a half months. Otherwise, nothing to read.

Nothing to do either, aside from making chains. To make chains all you have to have is bits of thread, a nail, and four pins. My mother brings all that back from her work, and that is how the two of us spend our long winter evenings when we are not outdoors in roll-call formation: I make up little chains that my mother sews into little doilies. I shall save one of them, made of dark material sewn with white thread. It will still be intact forty-eight years later, untouched by moths, its colors unfaded; lying on a coffee table, the effect will be very pleasant. It will safeguard the memory of all the tattered sweaters that furnished the material for it. It will attest to what, in the winter of 1944, was being worn from one end of Europe to the other. And people will ask, "A sample of Hungarian handicraft?"

The camp is very still. We speak quietly; to speak in a loud voice is tiring. On the other side of the fence the silence is yet deeper. The prisoners stand in silence, and when they collapse it is in silence too, without a word, without a murmur.

We are losing the notion of time. The days are all alike. It is difficult to say how long we have been here. Time no longer exists, even if we see the sun rise and night fall. The newcomers arriving from outside bring the date with them; but for that, *December, January,* or *February* would be words meaning nothing at all.

Friday evenings also help us to hold on to some notion of time, for the women try to light a candle if they can find one—which is rare and in any case strictly forbidden—or at least to say a prayer. They try also to respect the holidays, which is how I come to dread and to hate holidays, for on those days that are of particular significance to the Jews the Germans give us a little less to eat, forget the soup, reduce our ration of bread. On New Year's Day, 1945, they announce to us that henceforth rations are going to be trimmed further; that's our gift for the new year. We do not dare imagine what this new year will be like—still colder, no doubt, with a larger population in the camp, with an even greater hunger.

We know only too well that every exceptional occurrence is likely to bring something worse; we want no exceptional occurrences, our wish indeed is that nothing occur.

I do not know how we make our way through all that. It is like walking across a minefield, a mine every three yards, and keeping on and after each step ascertaining, without surprise and without joy, that you are still there, and finally, by a miracle, making your way through.

AT THE END OF THE LINE

Rumors trickle in, rumors spread. Several women are fluent in German, and while at work understand what they overhear Germans saying to one another. The two women who sleep with the Germans not only bring us bits of bread now and then but also a fugitive sentence or phrase heard over the radio. Newcomers arrive who have seen or heard something. So it is that we find out there has been a landing, without much knowing what that means. We hear talk of the Battle of the Ardennes: the Germans are in high spirits, it's a counteroffensive; once again they are defeating everyone in sight, they are unbeatable after all. We hear talk of the bombing of Dresden. We know that the British are approaching, that the Americans are not far away. We see airplanes, we see them fly over the camp without ever disturbing it. Do they know we are here?

Yes, we sense that something is coming. But we do not know that in a few weeks we shall be free. Oh, no. We do not believe that the war will soon be over. We cannot permit ourselves to believe it, or to dream about it, so much do we dread being disappointed. We have learned to protect ourselves against unpleasant surprises by envisaging worse, forever worse. We are in Bergen-Belsen, that is all we know, and we do not anticipate anything else.

And then all of a sudden, on the eleventh of April, the Germans start to evacuate the camp. The moment the evacuation begins, some among us are in a rush to set out without asking ourselves where they are going to take us. Others, including my mother and me, tell themselves that it is wiser to stay put for as long as possible. Our turn comes on the thirteenth; we are among the last to leave. Madame Jacobi, now mindful of her Russian origins, observes the ancient rite: before taking leave of our ghastly hut, with its quadruple-decker bunks, with its lice, she sits down and remains for a moment without stirring, silent, formulating a prayer—may the next place not be worse than this one. It is a supreme homage to Bergen-Belsen.

We are loaded into boxcars. There we find all those who set out two days before and who since then have been waiting in these freight cars, without anything to eat, for apparently they are not going to go to the trouble to feed us any longer. The Germans truly want to shut up shop for good, and as there isn't enough room for everybody, they add one more car, a coal car. In it are Berthe and the others belonging to the Lévitan group, very pleased to have air to breathe. The British are closing in on Bergen-Belsen. Though already surrounded on all sides, the Germans, even so, find a locomotive to pull our train.

The train advances, stops, sets off again. It proceeds thirty kilometers, halts, waits for who knows what, moves ahead a little, slows to a standstill. For four days it circles around the station at Celle, near Bergen-Belsen. For four days it changes direction incessantly; the British are coming from one side, the Americans from another; and after four days of travel we find ourselves three kilometers from the station we started out from.

Until the twenty-third, our train continues to trot about Germany. It heads in one direction, reaches a bridge that has been bombed, changes direction, and off we go again. It takes us through Hanover, it goes past Magdeburg. It goes three-quarters of the way around Berlin, turning clockwise all the time. It heads northward, then eastward, then to the south. We go through Potsdam. And we pursue our journey.

With each change of direction we imagine possible destinations. As in every group of people, among us there are optimists and pessimists. We speculate: the pessimists are confident that our guards have been given instructions to halt the train upon some bridge and to blow everything up—bridge, train, and deportees. The optimists think that we are going toward Theresienstadt, a camp that has the reputation of being a relatively mild place. The Theresienstadt legend has been transmitted to us by those who sojourned there or who have heard others talk about it, all with the nostalgia befitting a lost paradise. For anyone who once knew Theresienstadt, nothing is ever sufficiently good. Theresienstadt is the loveliest dream that the boldest among us permit themselves, a dream that approaches and withdraws in keeping with the train's changes of direction. The word *freedom* is no longer part of our vocabulary and no one pronounces it; the idea contained in it is too remote, incompatible with our condition, too vast. Theresienstadt, that's what we want.

Our cars are without any particular marking, and the soldiers guarding us know as little as we do about where we are headed. There are only a handful of them for the entire train, with their formidable police dogs. The men are old Wehrmacht guys, all somewhere in their forties, very little interested in knowing what is going to become of us, and not overly pleased to have been put in charge of us.

Now we come under attack from the air, several times. For the British, absolutely everything is a target. They pay no attention to red crosses; they know that the Germans paint them on military trains. The planes come over, the alert is sounded, the train stops, everybody clambers out. Sometimes we are bombed before a warning is given. On one occasion some people get themselves killed: not a bad way to go, all things considered. A burst from a machine gun comes so close to me that I am hit by the hail of pebbles it kicks up. So scared am I that even my diarrhea stops for a while.

The freight cars are not sealed. Some aren't even latched from the outside. One can slide the doors open and get a glimpse of what's going on. We halt every few hours, climb out to relieve ourselves and to steal anything we can get hold of. For at this stage we are being given nothing, really nothing, to eat. We lay hands on anything we are able to find in the fields, which, it being mid-April, is not much. We pull up nettles, we dig up the potatoes the Germans have just planted. We drink water from the ditches. And, of course, our diarrhea continues.

There is a moment of joy when during an alert we see, on the tracks next to ours, a gondola car filled with rutabagas: we climb into it and manage to serve ourselves copiously before our soldiers order us back into the freight cars.

Some die en route, but not many; others escape during the alerts, and they are not very numerous either. Berthe makes her escape in this way, runs off across the fields, hides in the woods. None of the women in her group reports her. I do not know what would have happened had she been among the others, in particular if the woman she had fought with had seen her run off: I doubt whether she would have resisted the pleasure of giving her away. And as Berthe is not in top form, they would have nailed her or quickly overtaken her, what with the dogs and all.

Berthe gets away, wanders for ten days, and at last runs into some French prisoners of war, who hide her and treat her very kindly. One of their number comes to see her and says to her: "My name is Lévy, Jean Lévy. My wife is in Bergen-Belsen. Do you know her by any chance?"

"Yes," Berthe replies, "yes, actually, I did know her, but I lost sight of her." Which is a lie, for Berthe knows very well that Madame Lévy died four days before the evacuation of the camp, weary of fighting to survive and ashamed of that weariness.

Yes, you could escape, some do. But for the most part we are too stupefied, too famished, too weak to attempt to do anything at all. We are wearing our camp pajamas, our feet are enveloped in rags, our bodies are covered with chilblains. Our hands are frostbitten, red, swollen.

Thus for ten days our guards try without much conviction to take us somewhere. On the evening of the twenty-second of April, we are in Tröbitz, near Torgau on the Elbe. All around us we hear shots being fired; the front is not far away. And during that night between the twenty-second and the twenty-third, our guards are forced to review the situation and come to the obvious conclusion: it is time for them to save their skins and avoid being caught with a train crammed with deportees. They abandon the train and go off. We are not aware of it; it happens while we are asleep. The next morning we discover that the train is no longer moving, and we see little Russian soldiers.

INTERLUDE

I am thirteen years old. On the twenty-third of April, 1945, at daybreak, the doors of our freight car are opened by Russian soldiers.

They understand at once that we are deportees and treat us with great gentleness. They do not appear at all discountenanced by the sight of the crowd of skeletons that we are. They help us down from the train and escort us to the nearby village of Tröbitz.

Many years later, just before dying, Jules, Aunt Alice's husband, will recount his deportation experiences to me. He had been liberated two weeks before I was, at Bad Tölz. All of a sudden the Germans had vanished, simply vanished; not a German in the camp, not one on the watchtowers. After what only seemed to be a long wait, the prisoners saw an American soldier walk up to the camp and then walk the whole way around it. Through the fence thousands of pairs of eyes watched his livid face and in thousands of minds there was the same thought: Is he about to faint? Isn't he going to need help? With great trouble the soldier pulled himself together, at least to the point where he was able to go off to get the others. The others in their turn seemed so shaken by the sight, so frightened to death, that the prisoners, Jules said, could not keep from smiling.

Well, our Russian soldiers have no problem of this kind. They grasp the whole thing, grasp it at once, life having no doubt well prepared them for it. They behave with great kindness but show no sign of emotion. It is only the former we are in need of.

Jules's Americans, distraught, overwhelmed by compassion, wanting to do good, unacquainted with famine, gave the prisoners everything they had, and they had a lot. With the rich American K rations, with the chocolate and the condensed milk, people fell like flies, suffering martyrdom, with perforations in their intestines, their stomachs. Even though certain deportees imposed rationing upon themselves and upon others, there were many dead on the day following liberation.

Our Russians, and this is a further instance of our incredible luck, have had wide experience with famine; they know the risk one runs after having spent a year on a diet like ours. They give us bread and good advice: be careful, take it very slowly, do not eat too much. Most of us, my mother included, listen to what they say; but certain others do not heed, overeat, and die the same day or the day after. A great pity.

Our sole thought, the priority of priorities, is to calm our hunger. We quickly learn that the word to say is *chleba, chleba,* which in Russian means bread. People rush in the direction of the village of Tröbitz, grab chickens, rabbits, wring their necks, make them into stews. It is very, very difficult to forbid oneself from eating, with this hunger gnawing as ferociously as ever.

Fortunately, my mother imposes a pretty strict discipline on us. Perhaps her Hungarian origins have something to do with it, perhaps she knows about the treacherous effects of prolonged famine. We eat very little at the beginning, just a small amount of bread, a few sips of broth. A Russian soldier takes me to Tröbitz, we enter a German house, go down into the cellar and clean it out. I make off with a whole basketful of jams and preserves. But we remain very cautious, my mother and I; we set it all aside for later.

The one thing preoccupying us, the one thing we are interested in, our one duty is to keep alive. To survive in Bergen-Belsen and to die now, like those people who stuffed themselves during the first days, would simply be too stupid. I apply myself to being sensible.

We are billeted with the inhabitants. All the sick are installed in a school. There are a good many of them, for there is typhus and many other diseases. Fortunately for us, the Russians are accustomed to want and sickness. They care for us exceedingly well, even if we are doctored with old wives' remedies rather than with medications.

How much time will it take for us to understand that our ordeal has come to an end? A great deal. We are unwilling to believe it. Our minds are not at rest, the Germans may still stage a successful counterattack.

No, liberation for us is not joy; it is a sort of confused relief. To be free—it doesn't strike us as so amazing. It doesn't strike us as so anything. We have learned to take things as they come. We're free? Fine, we're free. There's more to eat? We are indeed eating more. And what about after that? What are we in for next? We'll be finding out pretty soon.

Twenty-four hours out of the twenty-four all we do is simply try to survive. We are making no plans, we aren't doing any dreaming. If someone yields to his desire to move forward more rapidly than events are doing, we bring him back down to earth, saying to him, "I'll believe it when we get there, I'll believe it when I see it." For now the condition of survival is not to get excited, not to anticipate, not to expose oneself to disappointments. We are not in solid enough condition to withstand a disappointment.

We remain three months in this village of Tröbitz, in a sort of convalescence. What do we do during these three months? Nothing. We eat, we get a little better. However, there are some who die on account of one thing or another.

One day we hear that the Russians have come upon a tank car full of condensed milk left behind by the Germans. We are by now able to eat, our stomachs can cope with richer food. We sit down to a feast. We drink that milk and each swallow fills us with life. Some of it we set aside for another time. We have the stuff all over us from head to foot. Our hands are sticky from it, we have it all over our bodies. I don't know if there is anything in the world stickier than sweetened condensed milk. There's so much fat in it that it won't come off with cold water; it calls for the soap we obviously do not have.

The Russians are there with their little carts drawn by their little horses. Into them they pile whatever they happen to pinch, that is to say, everything, everything they can lay hands on. In their view, just as in ours, the Germany of 1945 is a land of the most delightful plenty.

They are as a rule aware of who we are. Some Russian officers speak German, others speak Yiddish; there are among us women of Russian or Polish origin who speak some amount of Russian. But among these soldiers and these officers there are all sorts: there are illiterates who understand nothing about anything; there are some who, hearing us speak German, are convinced that we are Germans, that is, German prisoners.

We know that they have already singled out some Germans and packed them off to no telling where. There's a strong chance that we, too, will find ourselves packed off to some part of Russia should that be somebody's decision.

For, yes, we are in the Russian zone. We have got to get back to France. But how? Set off on foot, walk the whole way? Continue to wait for them to come to fetch us? As in every kind of group, leaders appear. They start parleying, explain that we are not Germans, try to get some Russian officers to talk to the Allies about us, to find a French officer, to make it known to him that we are here.

As bellies are more amply filled, there is a steady quickening, a return of our sense of community. We begin to think of others, to aid one another, to do little things on each other's behalf, to talk to each other; little by little we become humans again. We quickly learn not to leave the women alone because there are Russians who want to rape them, something the women find comical, something that amazes them, poor souls, almost as much as it frightens them, for not only do they continue to look like skeletons, but they still feel as if they were halfway dead. They have forgotten that their bodies could present any interest whatever. At one point we are living with two French families, that is to say, with two women and their children. One of these women is of Polish origin. On the day of the armistice, the eighth of May, a band of completely drunken Russians shows up with the aim of raping the women—my mother, among others, who is frankly in too weak a condition to be raped, and the two other women, who are perhaps somewhat less skeletonlike but in no state to be raped either; they simply would not survive. Luckily, the Polish woman speaks Russian and succeeds in getting them to exercise a little patience. I don't know what she tells them, but a sort of negotiation ensues. The children dash off to get the officer. He arrives in time and orders all the soldiers out of the house.

That officer speaks a little German, a little Yiddish; the Polish woman understands Russian. It is he who informs us that the war is over. He is both happy about it and sad, because every one of his numerous kinsmen has perished under the occupation; he is the sole survivor. He is a Ukrainian Jew. When later on I shall hear Babi Yar spoken of, it is of him I shall think. "You have got to understand my soldiers," he says to us.

"They are perhaps not always very nice, but believe me, life has not treated them nicely either." He talks to us of the bombing of Dresden. He tells us that Dresden is a ruin, a heap of bricks and stone, a city not only deliberately killed but hacked to bits, massacred, smashed into little pieces, pulverized. "I know that it cost innocents their lives," he says, "but I do not at all regret that this bombing took place."

We continue to wait for the French to take cognizance of the fact that we are here. The hunger we endured becomes distant, a memory. But we do not abandon our old habits for all that, and continue to put aside pieces of bread for a later time.

I believe that it is owing to Berthe and to two other women who escaped from our train that the French learn of our existence. They talk about our convoy, a hunt for us begins, and we are finally found. We see a French officer drive up one day. He counts us and then leaves, promising to be back. Whereupon our wait becomes more precise and almost more difficult.

He returns three weeks later with American army trucks and has us get aboard them. It is late June. From Tröbitz we are taken first to Leipzig. Leipzig is not a pretty sight, but we don't mind in the least; far from it, we say that they have nothing but what they deserve.

After that we continue on in the direction of France. We drive through the American zone, then the French. With us we transport sacks full of pieces of stale bread. In Strasbourg they dust us with DDT in case we happen to have lice—and perhaps we do indeed have some. We reach Paris at the end of June and see with our own eyes that the world we left behind a year and a half ago still exists. We are given lodgings at the Hotel Lutétia, which constitutes a rather unexpected change of surroundings. But experience has prepared us for anything. Our big sacks of bread crusts are greeted with hilarity from all sides, because even if in Paris one doesn't find much to eat, no one has any use for the dry bits and pieces of stale German bread that we have been dragging about with us since God knows when.

Upon returning, we make a tally. We were three hundred when we left Drancy; one hundred fifty of us have come back. Exactly half.

AWAKENING

Thirteen years old. At Menthon-Saint-Bernard, on the edge of Lake Annecy, my preoccupation for the moment is to learn how to swim.

We are here as convalescents in a big and very comfortable hotel that the Ministère des Anciens Combattants has requisitioned for deportees. We are well looked after and well fed. We do not want for anything, which is far from the case for almost everybody else in France during the summer of 1945.

I spend two months at Menthon-Saint-Bernard with my mother, my father, and my Aunt Alice, who is in our company even though she herself was not deported. We already know what befell the others. We know that a part of my family disappeared in the camps, and once again we are made to realize that we were fortunate.

While in the camp I developed mentally. All sorts of things were pounded into me without my being able to say just what I did and did not learn. Physically, however, I did not evolve at all; rather, I regressed. At Menthon-Saint-Bernard I am the same height I was two years ago, and I weigh a lot less. The doctor examines me and seems concerned. "This child," I overhear him saying to my parents, "should already have reached puberty. Let's hope that it will happen shortly, but I truly do not know how this is going to work out." I am not too affected by this, as if I know in advance that everything was going to be just fine. On the other hand, the Jacobi children, one of them a year older than I am and the other two years older, will have serious problems. It is a good thing, so it appears, that I was only eleven when this business began and not twelve or thirteen.

In the course of their six years of separation, my parents each endured unimaginable experiences. The relationship they resume now is the very same one they had before; they pick up exactly where they left off. They get on neither very well nor very badly. For my father, all this about our deportation is without rhyme or reason; concerning it he is without the slightest curiosity, he is totally unaware of what happened to us. It's almost as if he were pretending to believe that none of it was worth writing home about.

I am seeing that people do not change much no matter what happens. My mother was always the worrying kind of person, critical and negative; she is even more so now. Back from the camp, my Aunt Aranka is just as solemn, doleful, and pessimistic as before. And my Aunt Boriska, who in my recollections was a lively young woman, charming, merry, who used to make bouquets of flowers that were like paintings, has come back more charming than ever and has started right in again composing her little bouquets. No, people have not changed, not underneath; at the very most, the camp has exacerbated certain features of their personalities.

My father, too, has returned the way he was when he left, equally disposed to angry outbursts and to laughter, unsure of himself, weak. He wasn't a grown-up when he went off to war; he isn't a grown-up now. He will die without having grown up. Before the war he used to be my best pal, who loved to play with me, who would take me to the movies every Saturday. Now I almost feel older than he is, and some of the things he takes pleasure in seem very puerile to me. To be sure, I'll sometimes skinny my way onto the metro without paying, sneak into the movies with five or six of my friends and only three tickets between us, and I'll be proud of myself for doing it. Yes, I shall perform such stunts from time to time, because those are among the games kids play and I am a kid. My father will seem to me too big for that sort of thing, and I will feel embarrassed at seeing him dodge past the conductor. It will make me uneasy to know that he hooks everything he can, postcards, candy, pencils, whatever. If he is not a total kleptomaniac, he's not far from it. He has diabetes and sugar is forbidden to him. But we are fully aware, my mother and I, that he hides candy in cupboards, stolen candy no doubt, and that he eats it when no one is looking. He is secretive, a sly-bones, won't express himself. Thoroughly a kid.

My children will adore him. They'll say that it's he who taught them how to laugh. He will tell them crazy stories, tall stories, and untruthful stories. They and he will have their secrets together, they will be confederates, they will be close to one another. But for my part, I look down on him a little, I do not take him seriously. For a good ten years after his death, I shall have frequent dreams of him. They will be sweet and pleasant dreams in which my father will simply be there, relaxed and happy in a general way.

As for myself, I do not have the impression I have changed much; it seems to me that all the camp did was reinforce what I would have been anyhow. Finally, though, how is one to know? Is it the camp that taught me to keep my own counsel, or did I already have, before I got there, an underlying guardedness, a distrustfulness? Can this be ascribed to the atmosphere that reigns in the house? Even after the war my father will not want it to be known that we are of foreign extraction. We will speak Hungarian when we are together, but in public that will be strictly forbidden; French will be obligatory. Nor will my father want it known that we are Jewish. We must conceal it from everyone.

Something splendid takes place at Menthon-Saint-Bernard: Aunt Alice meets Jules. Both are nearly forty, both are unmarried, and it's love at first sight, it's terrific, it's wonderful. And it will last for forty years, until Jules's death. In the course of their first encounter, they discover they are both of Hungarian origin, start speaking Hungarian to each other, and become inseparable.

For me, too, it's love at first sight: Jules becomes my idol, my idol forever.

It is Jules who teaches me how to swim, as he will teach me—or at least will attempt to teach me—many other things in the years to come. It is Jules who will be my model of strength and of rectitude.

Although it was with my mother that I was deported, although it was with her that I survived Bergen-Belsen, it is Alice and Jules who will school me and bring me up. It is Alice I shall choose for a mother and love as if I were her son. For I shall cut one by one all the ties connecting me to my own mother, as if I were obliged to punish her for the unbearable promiscuity of the Bergen-Belsen days, for the pieces of her bread that I ate, for what I knew to be her thoughts, for the bitterly cold nights when, clinging to each other, we had to share the slight amount of heat our bodies gave off. It is from Alice I shall learn how to live and how to think; it is she who will provide me with a certain self-confidence and who, above all, will free me from that hatred, from that distress, from those wounds of which I would perhaps not have been able to rid myself all alone.

Jules is suffering from a hernia, he is being cared for, he will be operated upon the following year. Jules's hernia is a very special one. I shall not find out about it until years later, when for the first and only time, shortly before his death, he tells me about the four and a half years he spent in Drancy, in Ottmuth, in Schoppenitz, in Birkenau, in Auschwitz, in Dachau, and in Bad Tölz. I shall learn then that he already had this hernia at the time he was arrested, that he was wearing a truss when he got to his first camp, and that he had the presence of mind to take it off before the initial lineup, for at muster the Germans would sort people into two groups, the weak on one side and those capable of working on the other. Thus, when they got to him, he was directed to the good side. Thereupon his hernia disappeared. For the ensuing four and a half years, he lifted stones that were too heavy, built the railroad, pushed wheelbarrows, demolished the ruins of the Warsaw Ghetto, and his hernia gave no sign of life. But a few weeks after his return to France, the hernia returned too, as though it had never gone away, for, evidently, not only people's nature but even the nature of hernias does not change in the camps. At Menthon-Saint-Bernard, Jules is once again wearing his truss while he waits to recuperate to the point where he can have his operation.

Jules plays chess. He reads and rereads, from the first line to the last, the speeches in which new members are welcomed into the Académie Française; the elegance of the style, the music of the splendid language fills him with wonder. He refuses, once and for all, to pick up a hammer or touch a nail; never again will he do any gardening or repair work around the house. He is a little man, very neat, very fastidious. He eats very little, very carefully selects what he eats, is almost obsessive in the matter of quality. A single string in a helping of string beans and he stops eating. One can imagine what a camp means for someone who has high standards as to the quality of life.

He is a dignified and orderly man who attributes enormous importance to work. He will one day say to my son, who will be spending time in Paris without quite knowing how to live there: "Do something. Study, work, it doesn't matter what it is, but do something. Idleness means the loss of dignity." To me he will say: "Lucien, you are out of your mind. You must calm down a little, stop rushing about, traveling all the time. You are an adult now." To my wife: "Have enough good sense for two."

I shall always regard Jules as a remarkable person. Slight, physically very frail, it is probably because of his low rate of metabolism that he survived in a place where big men with their big caloric requirements dropped like flies. But above all, it is because of his will to survive: if something could aid him to survive, he would do it, whether that meant digging holes, pushing wheelbarrows, or a piece of trickery. In that concentration camp world without social rules, a core of humanity always gathered around Jules. He had so much vitality, so much spirit, that he kept the others upright, infected them with his will to live. He was probably one of those likely to give up a piece of bread in exchange for a cigarette, for though he required both in order to survive, within that perspective his head was far more important than his body.

At the end of August we are back in Paris, and a little while later I return to the Lycée Buffon. We soon pick up our erstwhile routine; we resume a normal life. We are in our old apartment, everything is as before, except that now my father is with us and my mother does not work anymore. I am halfway up the stairs to get the mice I left with my neighbors when I decide not to do it. For I have other pets: I have a guinea pig, I have some frogs.

I skip the sixth form and enter the fifth. In all, this business has made me lose only one year. I have a craving to learn. I rediscover the joys of learning, as though starved after this long period without reading anything, without studying anything. The last intellectual nourishment I had came to me from Loève; after that I had nothing beyond impressions, observations, dreams, occasional things to do. The last, the very last thing I learned was the algebra Loève taught me. And now, as it happens, we are starting algebra in the fifth form, and I discover that I have an aptitude for mathematics, an aptitude that shall remain with me. I want to become normal again as quickly as possible, to adapt myself as quickly as possible, and I start right in. Making up a year of lycée isn't necessarily very easy, but I like schoolwork, I want to be first in my class, I want to be the best, and I succeed.

I know that one must live in the present, leave behind what lies behind. I am faithful to the principle I discovered in the camp: don't dwell on things too much, don't analyze them too much. I don't even have the time for that: I study, I go out with my lycée schoolmates, I make some friends, I begin to become interested in girls, I spend my vacations with Jules and Alice.

It's as if a parenthesis had closed. I believe that we are all trying, not just my mother and myself but every one of the hundred and fifty who have returned, to break with the past, to break with it as rapidly as possible, to assume again the habits we had as free people, to say to ourselves that it was a bad moment, that it's over with, that we must now turn to a new page. It is not our wish to forget Bergen-Belsen, but neither do we want to relive it. Instinct of self-preservation, I'm sure. We very soon lose sight of one another. After Menthon-Saint-Bernard I shall never again see the Jacobi children with whom I exchanged tattered sweaters; or the children of the Polish woman with whom I ran off to get the Russian officer when his men were about to rape our mothers; or Fernande of the ready laughter, to whom I am indebted for the most vulgar expressions I know. And, to my knowledge, Berthe has never sent her husband to see that amiable woman who ran a brothel.

Berthe will prove to be the only Bergen-Belsen acquaintance we remain in touch with, and that simply because she is a neighbor who lives only two steps away. Our friendship with Berthe will last for many years. Only after we have returned will it come into being, in the 14th arrondissement, for in the camp we barely knew each other.

We do not keep the promises we made ourselves while there, such as feasting on rutabagas with beet sauce and that sort of thing. We have forgotten them.

To do otherwise is dangerous, of this I have proof in the person of a second cousin. He was never deported. He and his wife managed to hide throughout the entire war. They were afraid the whole time. For too long they lived in fear of those very things I lived through. They are now quite unbalanced, both of them, fit to be institutionalized. At all hours of the day and night they hear "official communiqués" coming from everywhere. One has no sooner stepped out of the house than the other, panic-stricken, rushes to friends' homes in search of him, leaving a message like

"I have just got a communiqué, they're looking for us, it's official, we must move somewhere else, we must go into hiding this minute." A few years later it will have sent them to their graves.

I did effectively mention to two or three persons that I had been deported. They were greatly surprised; at such a tender age? I have come to see that this subject does not elicit people's interest, so I no longer bring it up. In the camp we were already saying to one another that when we got home nobody would believe us. It's true: whenever I recount some little episode, a scrap, people look at me incredulously. They doubtless have stories of their own which seem more important to them than mine.

Twenty-five years later Jules's daughter Evelyne will wake in the middle of the night seized with terror. For three years she will have nightmares that will paralyze her existence, nightmares about war and about concentration camps. Berthe's son will be a painter, especially highly thought of—to make the story somewhat funnier—in Germany. He will always paint oval faces upon incredibly thin oval bodies, like the bodies of deportees; all his pictures will be of ovals, crowds of debilitated ovals. Berthe, who has neither fondness nor respect for religion, will raise her son as an atheist. But Berthe's granddaughter, separated from Bergen-Belsen by a generation, will have nightmares just as Evelyne will have them in her time, will learn Hebrew, and with a scandalized Berthe as witness will cleave to an almost fanatical Judaism, so powerful will be the need to avenge oneself for Bergen-Belsen. And my own children, too, each in his own manner, will foot the bill.

As for myself, memories of deportation will never interfere with my sleep, nor will they will keep my mother or Berthe or Jules from sleeping.

I am alive. It makes little difference whether it really happened or whether it was just a bad dream. I am alive. That is all that counts.

HERE AND NOW

However improbable it may appear, I am already sixty years old. Not quite sixty, but almost. Once again I am in Paris, and once again I am living in a calm and pleasant neighborhood. The wars are all far away. I am not in danger of anything, apart from an accident, an illness, or—a rather unlikely eventuality—a treacherous passion. I am in control of all the rest.

I have found an attentive ear and I am talking about my hardest years, sometimes startled by what I find myself saying. To be sure, there is a risk in reopening that chapter of my life, the risk of failing to make myself understood, of repeating what everybody knows, which has been said and said better a thousand times already. But I have my reasons for taking this risk—which is not, after all, a very great one.

It wouldn't work in the United States, I wouldn't be able to talk about it there; and the proof is that in thirty years I have never done so, not once. This story belongs to Europe and to Europe alone. It is absurd more than anything else; its absurdity is of a species not found on the new continent. That is perhaps the reason why I emigrated and established myself in Arizona: not because of all the practical considerations—of which I drew up such a long list at the time—but in order to find myself in a world whose past is incompatible with mine, a world where a story like mine is inconceivable.

The tape recorder is running. I am in an apartment that is full of light, calm—with a hint of the free and easy. Two comfortable armchairs invite me to sit down for a long time. There are almost always freshly cut flowers about, and I soon get into the habit of bringing them here myself, so strongly does it seem to me that they belong and are almost indispensable here.

At first this well-mannered apartment did not seem like the appropriate place to broach confidential matters. Dramas are not at home in such surroundings. The starving, the humiliated, and the beaten soon notice that they strike the wrong note. This is not a place where one comes in order to die.

I plant watchtowers here, I string barbed wire, I make black famine reign; here I devote myself to a struggle for survival, mindless of the fate of others. The flowers start to wilt. I drag past carts filled with naked corpses drawn by reeling human horses, I bring down a rain of body lice and crabs. I repeat, astonished by the precision of this memory, the words spoken in an ever feebler voice by Madame Lévy, who expired four days before the camp's evacuation for want of hope and the will to live, Madame Lévy who, full of shame, begged us not to tell her husband: "I am letting myself die. I have given up all hope. I don't want him to know that."

At the beginning I am all but smitten by remorse, but by and by I see that this apartment's calm is only a seeming calm. I can tell there are phantoms lurk about, whispering their indictments and their advice, coming ever more alive as I recount my story. They suffer from the silence maintained around them, and the reception they give me and my dead could hardly be more favorable. I would say that they fairly feast upon my words.

I am told that I seem to be free of all hate and of all rancor. That rather surprises me, but having scrutinized myself, I do not find those feelings in my heart. If it is to please me, the Nazis who are still alive can die some unspeakable death, and the sooner the better. All those who have already died a preferably violent death, by drowning or hanging, all the Eichmanns and the Mengeles, deserved it not just once but a hundred times over. All right. But I wouldn't waste my time prosecuting them; that would be to do them too great an honor; I would not devote one minute of my life to them. Once upon a time I had all the hate in the world for the SS, the SA, all the contempt in the world for the kapos who made more of their job than they needed to, and almost as much for the population behind them who had so opportunely shut their eyes. But who knows? What if they had put me into a uniform as they did my friend Erich, who is two years my senior and who was in the Hitlerjugend? What if they had told me I belonged to the master race, told me the world was mine, and now forward march? I would perhaps have marched, there's no knowing. I would perhaps have said to myself that it's interesting, this stuff they're telling me, it's terrific, this feeling of pride they give me, this immense destiny they are promising me.

Over and above that I have to say I don't much like Germany. I do not have a good feeling there. But it is Germany's cooking that I do not like, its way of life, the hours the stores are open. As for the rest, I have always encountered people in Germany who have the same view of things that I have, and I allow the Germans to possess all sorts of qualities. I admire their efficiency even if I am not certain that I like it. They work very well; they have an excellent educational system that, as a professional, I know how to appreciate.

Yes, it is possible that I am free of hate and rancor. As evidence there is the fact that I went to Germany and worked there for some time. Also, my first child was born in Germany.

I have American cousins who, of course, did not undergo deportation. They cultivate that hate of the Germans and transmit it to the younger generation. Never would they buy a German-made product: not one toy, not one automobile, nothing. Japanese products maybe, but not German. They were very angry indeed when I went to Germany to work.

In 1958 I took a job with Renault. After a whole series of courses of instruction, I was put into the company's technico-commercial branch and sent to Cologne. The work was not unpleasant, the living conditions were distinctly better than in France, and the whole thing could have been quite all right. I could have continued my career as a technico-commercial engineer. But one day my French boss asked me where I had learned German so well; and out of defiance, or simply because I did not choose to hide it from him, I replied that it had been in Bergen-Belsen. Which wasn't even entirely true, for I had learned German grammar and enriched my German vocabulary at the lycée. "This is exceedingly awkward," said he. "This must absolutely not become known to anyone around here." He said it as if I had done something dishonest, committed a felony, or been concealing a shameful disease. And a few weeks later I was transferred to France. I found myself in a research laboratory in Billancourt, a good laboratory; the only trouble was that living conditions were very trying. We were unable to find suitable housing, getting to and back from work was an ordeal, and our parents were a little too close by.

In Cologne we had rented a furnished apartment, and it was overflowing with what were plainly stolen goods, objects confiscated from deportees like ourselves, in France or somewhere else in Europe, maybe packed up for shipping by the Lévitan people or, who knows, by Berthe. The closing of the absurd circle, so to speak. There were curios, wedding presents in sterling silver, furniture in the Empire style—none of that tallied with the wholly petty-bourgeois lady who was its proprietress. There was a painting of pensive rabbis shown studying the Talmud. What was the picture doing in the apartment of a lady who had the mug of a Nazi? I decided, in a moment of anger, that this painting was not where it belonged. When I heard I was being transferred, I wrapped up the painting and took it back to France with my things. In each house we have lived in since, it has had the place of honor. It is the one article of plunder I have from the war, well-deserved plunder, for, after all, I am one of the winners of that war. The owner went to my boss and complained, and even wrote to us demanding that we return her property; altogether pleased and proud of myself, I replied that I couldn't make out what she was talking about and that I did not recall having seen the picture in her apartment.

I am, I have always been, a very busy man. I contrive to have too much to do rather than not enough. I always have a text with me to correct, I always have a problem to resolve, telephone calls to make, a train or a plane to take, some students who are expecting me, some associates who are growing impatient. I see nothing of interest in lazy vacations or in holidays.

I am eager to live. I have a passion for living. The fact of having vegetated during a year and a half has given me an unappeasable desire to act and to learn. Given my age, given my situation, I could tell myself that it is not worth exerting myself this way, that it is time to stop. Nevertheless, I go on learning. No doubt I have an innate, natural curiosity, but Bergen-Belsen only strengthened it, of that I am sure.

Monday mornings I have my class on fuzzy multicriterion modeling at Paris VI. In front of me I have students trained in a different manner of thinking from the one I am proposing to them, students a little hostile to what I am talking to them about. They would prefer a more closely structured, more formal course; they are loath to strike out at random as I am inviting them to do. I present problems to them which have been solved with fuzzy logic and which could not be dealt with by any other approach, for fuzziness, imprecision, lies at the very heart of those problems. I tell them that the Japanese are right now forging ahead in the domain of fuzzy logic, that they are making machines operate and are running businesses in accordance with fuzzy logic; and their reply to me is that they are still skeptical even if the Japanese are excited. I find a certain narrowness in their outlook on life and in their way of conceiving of research. They are young, they ought to play for high stakes and not behave like small-time investors, looking only for sure bets from which there isn't a great deal to win.

My class ends at noon, I have lunch with Erich, and while we are eating we jot down notes for the colloquium we have to organize in the next few months. I race to the metro. I get to the Gare du Nord in time, three minutes before the departure of the train for Brussels.

I shall be in Brussels at five o'clock this afternoon. I have three hours in the train for reviewing the presentation I shall give in Brussels at six. I have the whole thing ready in my head. I need only scribble a few notes, turn one or two details over in my mind. But I have given courses on this subject so often and am so used to speaking to the widest variety of audiences that I see no harm in striking up a conversation with a blond sitting next to me. Instead of preparing my talk, I begin to chat with her and to turn on the charm. Then a point is reached where the blond begins to wear on me. She has by now told me everything she has to tell, or else, all things considered, I prefer to work on the talk I am to give in Brussels, and I go back to scribbling notes.

I give my talk. It all goes very nicely, our gathering ends at nine, and we stroll about Brussels for a while.

The next day I get together with Jean-Jacques, and we sit down to draft the article on the work we have just completed. At noon I call Paris and ask my cousin Evelyne how she is getting along. She is fine, she says, and invites me to dinner. I go to my two o'clock class, which lasts until four. On the train there is no blond to be seen, which allows me to write some letters. From the station I go directly to Evelyne's, without stopping at my place. I remain in Paris on Wednesday and on Thursday morning. I teach a class in which the students, while very nice, somewhat lose their bearings in fuzzy logic. I go over to the Broussais laboratory, where I am working on some ways of applying fuzzy logic in medicine. Thursday afternoon I take the train for Lausanne. In Lausanne I work with my friend André, I buy chocolates for some ladies in my entourage, and I have a great time Friday night. I roll into Paris at ten o'clock Saturday morning; I have an appointment at ten-thirty with A. for the drafting of another article.

I arrive at A.'s with my suitcase, and even before I take off my coat I have begun to tell her the new idea for our work that came to me on the train. "Why, that's exciting," she says. "But if you were to quiet down for five minutes, would it be the end of the world?"

To tell the truth, I think that the answer is yes.

I seem to always be on the go, but I know how to stop also. It's simply that I don't like to waste time. It is interesting to do interesting things, I have this possibility, and I make the most of it. My specialty, systems engineering and decision-making under uncertainty and imprecision, has varied and numerous applications. Visitors come to lay all sorts of problems before me, and rarely do these problems fail to evoke a response from me. I have worked in the areas of hydrology, of medical diagnosis, of the destruction of waste products, and of corporate management. I have dealt with the risk of flooding in mines, with groundwater management, with earthquakes, with the karstic aquifer control in Transdanubia, with weather forecasting, with dry events in semiarid countries, with conflicts between industrial development and the protection of the environment, with histopathology, with the diagnosing of arterial hypertension, and with evaluating the gravity of cases of axonal peripheral neuropathy. It doesn't take much for my curiosity to be roused.

I like intellectual challenges, and I don't like to lose. I am very attached to my teaching activities. It is always upsetting to me when after a poor lecture I realize that my students did not latch on. I am furious when I see my graduate advisees unable, for lack of willpower, to complete their dissertations, choosing to hang around the university for years before finally leaving without anything in their hands.

I rather like doing several things at the same time. I don't much ask myself whether I am happy living in this way, since no other way would be bearable for me. I don't ask anyone to applaud me for that, neither do I ask permission to live as I jolly well please.

I believe that drives those close to me to despair, that they interpret it in a manner which sometimes dumbfounds me.

My impression is that my children have never accepted my way of living, that they have never understood why I have had to be on the move, to be at it all the time, to always be doing something. They have taken that as if it were directed against them, as if it were in order not to be with them. At the age of twelve my daughter knew that I worked at the university, but not that I was a professor there; she thought vaguely that I was at best some sort of administrator. And without knowing what I was doing, how could she have understood who I was and what I was feeling?

Yes, my children believed I was neglecting them, that I was not a good father, that for me work mattered more than my family. They think that to this day.

How do they judge my profession, the fact that I do research, that I teach? What value does that have in their eyes?

Not a very great one. Taking them by order of age, my older son has always, with regard to teaching, to research, to the university, shown an extreme hostility and scorn; he has beheld all that as useless, and all professors, or very nearly all, as jerks. When he saw a book with my name on the cover, he did indeed taste a brief moment, a truly very brief moment, of satisfaction.

My second son does seem to appreciate what I do, but he is not much impressed by it. He thinks there are more interesting and perhaps more respectable paths to follow. He is seeking one for himself. I cross my fingers in the hope he finds it, in the hope he does not undergo lifelong frustration.

My daughter did well in school, works well, has a very good rapport with her mother, tries to understand me. With her things are easier. But they are not without their undertones.

When I see the problems my children have in their affective relationships, I always say to myself that, well, I probably set them a bad example. I have committed serious mistakes and not known how to repair them soon enough. My slight talent for explaining myself, for expressing my feelings, must have had baneful consequences for those close to me.

It is hard for me to say it to myself. I am ready to apologize to them. I truly did not mean to hurt them, but I admit that I did so. What else can I do now but talk to them? And that supposes that they are willing to listen to me, that they do a little thinking afterward, and that they act. It is really for them to take their own lives in hand; it is up to them and no one else.

My children are Americans. They do not know that you have to be able to function under any regime, under all sorts of circumstances. They expect the world to be the way it ought to be, with the game played according to decent and well-respected rules, with the right recipe for living, with the real truth set forth somewhere. Our misunderstanding no doubt proceeds from the fact that I lost that sort of innocence at the age of eleven. I understood then, once and for all, that however disagreeable your circumstances, however far your parents are from being model parents, you cannot for one instant afford the luxury of being unable to function, you do not have that possibility, that option does not exist.

Other times, other ways?

Once, long ago, when the children were still small and when times were not easy, my wife found herself worn out, in despair, down with a cold, unhappy, everything at once. I said to her then: "You do not have the right to be sick." My God, did she take it badly! I realize now that every other woman would have found that unendurable, would have felt betrayed and not loved. What, I don't have the right to be sick? Oh yes, I do! I have the right to be sick just like everybody else! It was as if I had sought to reduce her to bondage, as if I had threatened her with a whip, obliged her to pull her galley slave's oar whatever it cost her. But that is not at all what I wanted to communicate to her. I should doubtless have expressed it some other way, but I believe that even so I would not have succeeded in transmitting to her my loathing, my dread, my refusal of sickness. That is perhaps cruel; but, truly, it is not desirable to be weak.

It is very likely that I have not managed to be a dad in the way one is supposed to be, and perhaps my children will one day say of me, as I say of my father, that "he never grew up, he was a boy till the day he died." It makes a very cruel epitaph. But that's not what saddens me, that's not what makes me uncomfortable. My discomfort comes perhaps from a feeling of injustice—though I am not in the habit of dwelling upon injustice—for in a certain way I am responsible for their problems, and it may be that through my gestures, my words, and, above all, my silence, Bergen-Belsen still seeks to inflict an ultimate defeat upon me by casting its shadow upon the lives of my dear ones.

I must dispel that shadow. Yes, after much thinking about it I say to myself that my children—and my wife still more so—ought to be made acquainted with my story, that I have been wrong not to have recounted it to them other than piecemeal, in snatches.

So here is the tale of what my eyes have seen, of what my memory has retained. Once it has come into their hands, may they make what use of it they can.

Lovingly,
Lucien

Afterword

Since the French publication of *Lucien's Story*, I have met many of its readers, all of whom were curious to know what lay behind this book, how and why it was conceived and came into being. So here is its history, such as it stands in my memory.

It all began in Fort Worth, Texas, during a conference of scientists that Lucien Duckstein and I were both attending. Experienced participants know that impromptu discussions and personal contacts entered into at conferences of this sort are sometimes more interesting than what is on the official program. Certain of these contacts are maintained and eventually open the way to serious and fruitful collaboration. That is what happened in this case—thanks, it is true, to two favorable circumstances. The first was of a practical nature: Lucien was in close touch with a Paris laboratory and came to Paris regularly, at least once a year. In the second, sentiment was the essential element: between us there was a kind of affinity, for we both belonged to the vast nation of exiles, between whose members, wherever they have come from and wherever they settle, there is, upon certain subjects, an implicit understanding. For it soon came out that Lucien, besides being a professor at the University of Arizona, was also French and a Parisian by birth; as for me, although a researcher in a French laboratory, a French citizen installed in Paris, I was in essence a Polish immigrant and nothing else.

But if we continued to remain in touch, if our contacts gradually turned into a solid professional friendship, it was largely for one very practical reason: from the outset the advantages of a collaboration had been evident to us. I work in the medical domain, and now and then I run into problems that defy the usual approaches. This, at the very time our first meeting occurred, had led me to peer in the direction of what mathematicians have come to call fuzzy logic, which seemed to hold out certain new possibilities. For his part, Lucien, then mastering fuzzy theory and techniques, was on the lookout for a new area in which to apply them. Thus, over the course of a few years, Lucien was for me a colleague and a teacher. I felt I was fortunate, and not because of his professional qualities alone. Lucien possessed a contagious enthusiasm, a joyful way of confronting, of surmounting, or of circumventing difficulties, an insatiable appetite for fresh challenges. Work undertaken with Lucien would go well, and it would go forward enveloped in good humor and a kind of state of grace. Whatever your profession, I have perhaps said enough for you to understand that when one comes upon such a collaborator, one cherishes and holds on to him. Consequently, upon learning that he was going to take a sabbatical and that he wished to spend part of it in Paris, I did all I could to get our laboratory to invite him.

But while I was well acquainted with the scientist Lucien, I knew almost nothing about his life, just as he knew almost nothing about mine. If at that time I had been asked to describe him, I would have spoken of a man at the height of his professional life; happy in his family life, husband of the elegant and very beautiful Aloha, whom I had a brief glimpse of one day in Paris, father of three children, Marc, Nicolas, and Sonja, of whom he was apparently very proud; a convivial, joyful man, with a touch of jauntiness about him. I would not have suspected any zones of shadow in his life.

Then one rainy day in November we were walking down a street in Paris' 14th arrondissement. I must stress that had this walk taken place in another city, in different weather, the conversation probably would not have taken the turn it did. But on that day, in that chill and grayness, the sidewalks beneath Lucien's feet spoke to him of paths followed half a century earlier. Streets shed their anonymity in order to become once again the street where the kindergarten had been, the one that led to the lycée, the one where the police station stood, in which he had spent his first night of captivity and in which at sunrise the weary gendarme had given him, as a good-bye present, a bowl of hot chocolate. Forgotten voices resonated anew amid the buildings, the dialogue resumed at the spot where it had been interrupted. Lucien was no longer an American professor spending a year abroad. The past came flowing back, the past that disquieted and hurt, for if Paris was where he had known his first happinesses, Paris was also the city of his earliest dreads, where he had met with his first painful experiences. At one of its corners the veil lifted ever so little, and I heard him say:

"I hate the month of November. It's the month of my worst memories. I was taken away to Drancy in November."

I stared at him, at a loss for words. After a moment Lucien added:

"That's right, I spent six months in Drancy. Then twelve in Bergen-Belsen."

It is hard to come up with an intelligent rejoinder when someone says to you, "I was in a concentration camp." Lucien was already having misgivings about confiding in me, a look of embarrassment had appeared on his face as though he had just committed a blunder, forgetting that it is not good form to talk to people about one's misfortunes, present or past. And as I detest prying, we were indeed within an ace of abandoning the subject once and for all. In another instant Lucien would be assiduously effacing the words he had blurted out, hiding them behind a smile, burying them beneath some anodyne remarks, and off again on one of our usual subjects of conversation. I said that I supposed that this was something he was probably disinclined to talk about.

"No," Lucien replied, rejecting my pity and dispelling the uneasiness that had taken hold of me. "No, I wouldn't mind. To the contrary. If I never talk about it, it's because it doesn't interest anybody. People don't want to know about it."

In the next few minutes we came to an agreement: he would recount his story for me, I would put it into written form, proceeding on the hypothesis that it could, after all, interest somebody. For my part, I was motivated not only by a keen feeling of injustice, but also by my fascination with a phenomenon that I wanted absolutely to explore: how had someone who had been put through the incredible traumas of a concentration camp been able to turn into the generous and smiling person I knew? As for Lucien's motives, I was not to discover them until later and only little by little, as I listened to his emerging story.

It could, of course, have gone no farther than that; we could have contented ourselves with the promise without ever proceeding to act upon it. But we were too much in the habit of keeping our professional commitments for that to happen. The two of us never engaged in idle talk together. And so, no more than three or four days after that conversation, Lucien came to my home, I poured him a drink and turned the tape recorder on right away, not so much in a hurry to begin but so that we might get ourselves used to the machine's indiscreet presence. Lucien thereupon asked me the question which set the tone for all that followed:

"Tell me, have you ever known hunger?"

After that, neither one of us could retreat, or would have wanted to.

So that is how this book was born, the result of a series of chance events, of wind and rain, of some exchanged glances, of a few imprudent words, which had revealed to Lucien the intensity of his desire to revisit a time now fifty years past and to defy the law of silence. It was born also from my deep regret at having again and again not known how to listen and to ask questions when it was yet possible to do so. But that has to do with my own memories; and my memories, you understand . . . they are another book. For in this one I have practiced a deliberate, scrupulous self-effacement before Lucien's story, Lucien's voice, Lucien's truth. My memories count only insofar as they enabled me to reply in the affirmative to Lucien's question as to whether I had ever known hunger, and to behold an incredible expression of relief on his face as he said, "Fortunately, for hunger is very difficult to explain to someone who has never undergone it." Here my memories have served only to the extent they caused me to recognize, with painful certainty, the irrefutable truthfulness of Lucien's story, to absorb his words, and to sense what questions needed to be asked.

Among my memories, however, there is one that deserves to be cited: a memory so distant, so intimate, that I hardly dare evoke it.

In another life, in another world, at a date I would not be able to specify, during that time when childhood is giving way to adolescence, I saw Auschwitz in the course of a visit organized by the school I was attending. Docile, we followed the guide into the huts and into the gas chambers, where there was so little headroom that the ceilings bore traces left by the fingernails that had raked them in the very last spasm of a still-struggling body. But we children were blasé. In my age group there were few who had never heard the wail of air-raid sirens and the din of exploding bombs, few in whose family there was no one to mourn. As defense against the horror of the Auschwitz camp, we had the conviction that the monsters responsible for it were no longer alive, that the war was something over and done with. Besides, our parents almost never talked about it in our presence, too anxious to see us rid of our nightmares, too taken up with finding food for us to eat, too eager to see smiles on our faces. We knew that once we had finished our tour of the camp we would find the real world again, the one waiting for us outside, where death was only an abstract notion. Auschwitz was already part of history.

Then we went into a shed where the guide showed us great heaps of objects taken from the prisoners, objects there had been no time to dispose of before the camp's liberation. Gazing at one of those heaps, the one consisting of toys, all my defenses fell to pieces. That sight was to haunt me for years, and it overwhelms me now even as I write. There were dolls, some very sophisticated ones, others very modest, all loved enough to have been carried along on that last journey. There were teddy bears, so soft to the touch that the children would hug them very tight so as not to be afraid in the dark night. There were toys for the littler ones and for the bigger ones, a multitude of toys; each one had been held in the hand of a child, and in letting go of it, the child was saying good-bye to life. What I felt then was no longer mere pity or circumstantial horror, but a paralyzing dread, a limitless indignation and weariness. Never has the world's cruelty appeared to me more sharply than at that moment.

But I was too young to abandon all hope. And so, for a long time, I dreamed that one of those children had survived, that there had been at least one to feel the caressing warmth of the sun upon his skin, to run in the forest, to play silly pranks, to read books, to love and be loved.

My prayers were answered. I met that child. His name was Lulu.

Aleksandra Kroh